Four Zulu War Correspondents & Artists

Four Zulu War Correspondents & Artists
The Personal Experiences of the Campaign by
Prior, Fripp, Forbes and Norris-Newman

ILLUSTRATED

Melton Prior

Archibald Forbes

Charles E. Fripp

Charles L. Norris-Newman

Four Zulu War Correspondents & Artists
The Personal Experiences of the Campaign by Prior, Fripp, Forbes and Norris-Newman
The Zulu War: 1879-80
By Melton Prior
Bill Beresford and His Victoria Cross
by Archibald Forbes
Reminiscences of the Zulu War, 1879
by Charles E. Fripp
and
Isandlwana and Rorke's Drift
by Charles L. Norris-Newman

ILLUSTRATED

FIRST EDITION IN THIS FORM

Extracts first published in the titles
Campaigns of a War Correspondent
Barracks Bivouacs and Battles
The Pall-Mall-Magazine 1900
and
In Zululand with the British

Leonaur is an imprint of Oakpast Ltd
Copyright in this form © 2023 Oakpast Ltd

ISBN: 978-1-916535-38-1 (hardcover)
ISBN: 978-1-916535-39-8 (softcover)

http://www.leonaur.com

Publisher's Notes
The views expressed in this book are not necessarily those of the publisher.

Contents

The Zulu War: 1879–80 *By Melton Prior*	7
Bill Beresford and His Victoria Cross *By Archibald Forbes*	53
Reminiscences of the Zulu War, 1879 *By Charles E. Fripp*	71
Isandlwana and Rorke's Drift *By Charles L. Norris-Newman*	101

Melton Prior

The Zulu War: 1879-80

By Melton Prior

On my return down country to King William's Town, (1878), I was fortunate enough to be present at a conference between General Thesiger and the different heads of the volunteer corps, well-known farmers, and Dutch and German Boers.

The conversation turned on the prospects of the Zulu War, as it was known that that nation was very disturbed.

The *Burghers* and Boers, who had fought the Zulus in days gone by, assured General Thesiger that any army fighting the Zulus would have to *laager* at every halt made after crossing the border. General Thesiger said, "Oh, British troops are all right; we do not *laager*—we have a different formation."

The Boers again and again assured him that it would be absolutely necessary, and that no column ought to halt for breakfast or dinner under any circumstances without *laagering*.

Again General Thesiger smiled at the notion, but I was very much impressed at the earnest and serious way in which the Boers explained the risk, and the necessity for this action. So firmly was I convinced that if General Thesiger, afterwards Lord Chelmsford, did command the British troops he would not take this sound advice and *laager*, that on my return to England, in conversation with Mr. William Ingram, I explained this matter to him, and said, "You take my word for it, if we do have a war with the Zulus, the first news we shall get will be that of a disaster"—and sure enough I was correct. We all must remember that the first serious news to reach England with regard to that campaign was the slaughter and almost anhilation of our column at Isandlwana.

I think I have said before in this book of reminiscences (*Campaigns of a War Correspondant*) that I cannot attempt to give a detailed description of the wars, but I think I may mention the cause which led to the conflict with King Cetewayo. He had not been provoked by the British Government; they had done their best to avoid trouble.

Ever since the days of Chaka, whose reign extended from 1810 to 1828, the Zulus have been regarded as the military race of South Africa. At the time of the war in 1879 King Cetewayo possessed a force of over 40,000 men well organised and fairly well equipped, the army being divided into regiments varying in strength from 400 to 2,000, each commanded by an *induna*, or chief.

In former years a bundle of light *assegais*, a short and heavy one for stabbing, a shield and a *knobkerry*, were the arms of the Zulu soldier, but now many regiments were armed with breech-loading rifles. In each case the stabbing *assegai* was still carried, but the shield was discarded.

In 1873 with the aid of some Europeans a small powder factory was established, and a magazine built at the principal military *kraal*, which was called Mainze Kanze, meaning "Let the enemy come now."

Matrimony was forbidden to the soldier, but periodically the king would order a whole regiment to marry, and to select for their wives the daughters of men belonging to some special regiment.

The strictest discipline was enforced throughout the army, cowardice on all occasions being punished by death. The women were in charge of the commissariat, and they would travel forty and fifty miles a day when carrying supplies to the army in the field.

The Zulu has an innate love of fighting, and firmly believes in his own invincibility. Such is the military character of the nation against whom we were about to wage war.

When the news of the disaster at Isandlwana reached England, a meeting of the Cabinet was hastily summoned, and it was then decided to despatch a strong force of infantry, cavalry, artillery, engineers, and army service corps men as reinforcements to the Cape. I was ordered out by my office.

There was a number of officers on board the s.s. *German*, hurrying out to Natal in consequence of the reverses we had received, amongst them Major Charles Bromhead, who had only been married two years, and who was going out to take up the command of the remaining few companies of the 24th Regiment which had suffered so severely.

It was his brother. Lieutenant Bromhead of the 24th, who, with Lieutenant Chard, R.E., won the V.C.—that much-coveted decoration—for their magnificent and heroic defence of Rorke's Drift. Their action no doubt saved Natal from invasion by the enemy.

I am now going to mention a subject of which I am not particularly proud. I had been through several campaigns, some of them very disagreeable ones. I had run many risks and fear had never entered into my mind, but unfortunately, on my journey out on this occasion, I had a bad dream. I call it a dream, but I think it must have been a nightmare. It took place after I had arrived at Durban.

Now this nightmare had such an effect on me that I have never forgotten it. I dreamed that I went with the relieving force to rescue Colonel Pearson at Etchowe. I saw myself shot, and I saw myself buried.

Strange to say, by the next mail arriving from England I received a letter from my mother, in which she told me she had had a dream that I had gone with the relieving column to Etchowe, that I had been killed, and that she had seen my funeral, and she wound up by begging me most earnestly not to go with that column, and it is now that I am ashamed to own that this had such an effect on me that I made up my mind I would not go, and even wrote to Mr. William Ingram at my office to inform him of my determination. Some weeks later I received a cablegram from him:

> Sorry you did not accompany force, no doubt saved for better things to come.

However, I did not wish the *Illustrated* to be unrepresented in this expedition, and I succeeded in enlisting the services of Colonel Crealock, the Chief of the Staff, and also engaged the services of a private individual named Porter.

Now comes the curious incident of this act of mine. When the fighting did take place, at Ginghilovo, on the road to Etchowe, my specially appointed artist was one of the first killed.

Whether I believe in presentiments may or may not be interesting to anyone, but this case is surely curious.

At the Royal Hotel I met a Mr. Walter Peace, who a few years after was appointed High Commissioner for Natal in England. He informed me he was going out to the Tugela, whence the troops were to start for the relief of Colonel Pearson at Etchowe. He had already engaged a carriage and offered me a seat, so I had an opportunity of seeing the troops and making a sketch of them starting on the expedition, and I slept that night in the tent of the commissary. General Strickland. He was very kind to us, and gave us breakfast, and then we started back, and I arrived once more in Durban, feeling rather ashamed of my want of pluck.

During the time that the column was operating for the relief of Colonel Pearson I was engaged sketching the arrival of fresh troops from England, and the many interesting scenes to be found in Durban.

The Post Office did not seem to be conducted exactly in a way that one would expect in a British colony. I was actually told seriously that I must register my sketches and photos, or they might not reach England, as the clerks were very fond of opening any parcel that they thought might be of interest, and in the case of my sketches it was quite possible for them to keep them; and I was also informed that I must register them eighteen hours before the mail left. On hearing this I went to the Union Steamship Company's offices, and they very kindly said they would put my sketches and any of the correspondents' letters in their private boxes which are taken direct to the ship sailing for England, and would thus avoid any risk of our letters being opened.

One day, going to the post office about a little matter, as a kind of test I asked the post-master how late I could post at his office, and he said at half-past six, "but be sure," he added, "that you put on enough stamps, as otherwise your letter will not go."

I stared at him in astonishment, and asked if he really meant what he said. "Do you really mean to say, sir, that if I put on a shilling stamp, and it is not enough by one penny, that my letter will not go?"

He replied, "Certainly not."

When I asked him what became of it, he replied, it would be put on some shelf and left. And this is how the Post Office in those days was conducted.

The other correspondents, on hearing this, devoted an article to the management of the post office at Durban, not much to its credit, I fear; but on representing this matter to headquarters things were soon put right.

As the time drew near for a move forward, we were informed that Lord Chelmsford had decided to issue military passes to the correspondents. This was the first time that such a thing, I believe, had been done, and one or two of the Press men were rather indignant and annoyed at this new regulation, but eventually we all realised that it would be really and truly for our benefit, for no outsider would be allowed to go to the front without this authorisation. We were asked to draw up a form of pass, which was eventually agreed upon, and accepted by the general. It was then printed, and as each was signed by him and handed over, he informed us smilingly that without it we might be sent back from the front as vagabonds under arrest.

As the reinforcements were arriving and going forward, the time had arrived when I had to decide whether I would go with the coast column or with that of General Newdigate, and I decided on the latter, as I heard Lord Chelmsford was going to accompany it.

The correspondents' trouble in these times is the same as a general's in regard to transport and commissariat. You must have luggage, you must have provisions, the difficulty is to know how to transport them. In this case a correspondent invited me to join him in purchasing a carriage and horses for our luggage. I had always made up my mind to be independent of anyone, but on this occasion, I gave way.

When, however, I saw the enormous amount of luggage that he crammed into the cart, even his steamer trunk, I was certainly well satisfied that this arrangement would not last very long. However, the cart was packed, and I sent it off in charge of my man George. He was to go by steady marches from Durban to Maritzburg, and was to wait for me, as I proposed going up to Pine Town and Bowker's Hill by rail, and thence on by post cart. The difficulty was to know what to do with my two riding horses. I called on the Chief of the Police, Captain Hannay, who was an Englishman, and a rare good fellow. I asked him if he could give me two of his police to lead them to Maritzburg, which was a distance of fifty-eight miles.

He said, "Well, Mr. Prior, if you take my advice, you will engage two raw Kaffirs. I am sorry to say my police are not to be depended on. They are simply rascals, every one of them. They would ride your horses all the way, let them eat grass, would not go near an hotel, and would thus rob you of their keep. Whereas, if you like I will send you two Kaffirs with their blankets, and you may depend on them to act honestly by you."

The following morning, they arrived. I gave them my horses, money to pay for their feeds at the hotels, and a promise of a certain sum for the journey.

On starting I had been careful to chalk the animals' backs and put my initials underneath the saddles, for it is an old dodge, if you chalk the top of the saddle, for the Kaffir to take it off the horse's back and ride the animal, carrying the saddle on his head.

Pine Town I found to be one of the most charming little country places I had seen in South Africa. This place had also been *laagered* and stockaded, as a precaution against the Zulu raid.

From Pine Town I took the train to Bowker's Hill, which is reckoned about half-way. In those days the trains took three hours to do thirty-three miles, and the post cart did the other thirty-five miles also in three hours. This does not say much for the speed of railway travelling in South Africa.

Just as I was getting into the post cart, four officers I did not know came up and requested me to get out, saying that I must wait until next day, as they had to go forward at once. My answer was, a smile. They were young, and rather rude, but when I produced my pass and my receipt for the seat, they were profuse in their apologies.

I found post-cart travelling here as bad as in Kaffraria—only a little worse.

Away we tore, up hill and down dale, all at the same pace, the driver sounding a horn nearly all the way. Across drifts and swampy roads that had been made good by branches of trees, when the driver would call out, and you had to hang on like grim death.

Sure enough, when I arrived at the Windsor Hotel at Maritzburg my two raw Kaffirs were already there, and they produced receipts from the different hotels they had stopped at on the road for food for themselves and fodder for the horses, and on examining the saddles and horses I found my initials intact.

My man informed me that he had had terrible trouble with the cart and luggage, so much so that I decided to alter the arrangement with regard to the other correspondent, and the following morning went in search of a cart for myself.

I found a second-hand dog-cart, for which I paid £25. I had it examined by a wheelwright, who charged me two sovereigns for pretending to do to it something which I could not see. He then pronounced it in good condition.

Archibald Forbes, that brilliant military correspondent of the *Daily News*, had arrived. I was highly delighted to meet him once more.

While chatting with him and some officers, I heard for the first time of the death of Major Hackett, of the 90th. I was awfully grieved, for he was such a fine fellow and had been so kind to me during the Kaffir War. It appeared that at the Battle of Kambula Hill, a bullet hit him on the left-hand side of the face, breaking the bridge of the nose, and carrying away both his eyes. This affected the brain to such an extent that when being treated by the surgeons he called out for the blinds to be drawn up, as he wanted to see.

In this horrible state he lingered for several weeks. Poor Hackett!

Having at last arranged to go forward to join General Newdigate's column, I had my cart packed with tinned provisions, wines, spirits, &c. The horses were put in. All was then ready for a grand start. There was quite a crowd at the hotel, standing outside to see me leave. My man had been accustomed to horses and driving all his life, and came out of the yard in great style. He was proceeding down the road, when all of a sudden, without any previous warning, and to my horror, I saw the cart turn completely upside down and all my chattels and goods go flying in all directions.

Away I ran, followed by a crowd, to find out what the reason was. I could not blame the man, for I had seen the collapse. On examining the cart, the cause of the accident was quite clear; one of the wheels was so rotten that it had given, and the bolts of the springs had also come away. This looked like a dead loss; however, I was not to be done. I went to a coach-builder and bought a brand-new buggy, for which I gave £40.

Once more we packed my goods, barring the broken bottles of whisky, and I made another start, this time with great success.

The main road from Maritzburg up country is one long, continuous hill of about four miles, and it took fully two hours to mount it.

What with driving the horses and pushing the cart, when we arrived at the top my man was pretty well done up. I found there was a little store there, and I asked him if he would like a drink. "Yes, please, sir." He said he would like a glass of beer best, so I told the storekeeper to bring a glass of beer, and to bring me some Hollands and water, better known as "Square-face" or "White Velvet," as Archie Forbes had nicknamed it. When it came to paying, I discovered that my drink was sixpence, but my man's four shillings, whereupon I gave him due notice that that was the last drink of beer he would have until he returned to Durban. Four shillings for a bottle of beer up country I found was the regular price, when it wasn't five shillings.

My little trip from Maritzburg to Ladysmith was carried out in this way:—

Howick	13 miles
Currie's Post	12 "
Mooi River	16 "
Griffin's Farm	14 "
Estcourt	8 "
Blaawkrantz	11 "
Colenso	10 "
Rising Sun	8 "
Ladysmith	16 "

At Ladysmith I set to work to finish up the sketches I had made on the road and went over to the post, when I was informed that the mail cart would not be able to start that day, as the driver had been found drunk, and as there was no one else able to drive the mail cart it would not be able to start until after he had become sober.

This sounds most extraordinary, but it is nevertheless a fact. This man, however, eventually drove the cart at such a pace that he picked up a whole day's journey on the road, and actually did save the mail boat at Durban.

At Ladysmith I was on the veranda of the hotel, smoking, when a bold and impudent young Kaffir on horseback, dressed in a smoking cap with gold tassels and white breeches and top boots, in fact got up generally in a most extravagant manner, and accompanied by four others, apparently servants, rode up in front of the hotel. Seeing some Kaffir that he knew, he called out in thorough English, and with a large amount of swagger, "God damme, damned hot. I'm just riding into the city. Can't stop to chat with you fellows now!" and with a jocular wave of the hand, put spurs to his horse and galloped on. One could not help smiling at this, because it was so evidently picked up from the Englishmen.

This was what is called a Christian Kaffir, for whom everyone has the greatest contempt. A Missionary Kaffir becomes a liar and a thief, whereas a raw Kaffir is one of the most honest men to be found in the world and the women are most virtuous. The hotel-keeper told me that one day he had been counting up money to send to the bank, and just as he had finished, he was called away suddenly, and left his cashbox in the bar. Later on, he shut up the house and went to bed, forgetting he had left the money. But he had not been in bed half an hour when one of his raw Kaffirs, who always slept in the bar, came to his door and tapped and made him get up, telling him he had left his money on the table.

"Come, master, come get it; some thieves might find it!" and when he went with the Kaffir he found it all there—not a penny of two hundred pounds had gone.

Now this man might have taken it all, run away, and never been seen any more; he could have bought cattle and wives and been a rich man for the rest of his life.

That same evening, about five o'clock, my boy came to me with a face as white as a ghost, and, in a terrible fright, said that he had lost my horses. He had knee-haltered them as usual, and let them loose to graze, and then suddenly he had lost sight of them. There is no doubt the young rascal had lain down on the ground, fallen fast asleep, and in the meantime his charges had wandered afar. I thought the best thing to do was to go to the magistrate and ask for some Kaffir policemen to search for them. He said it was impossible, as by this time it was very dark, but added they would be all right and perfectly safe until the morning. However, when the moon came up, my boy started out again up the hills and was away most of the night, but without success.

Suddenly the idea occurred to me that they might have gone over to join the artillery and cavalry horses, so I told him to go over and have a look for them there, and after a tramp of about five miles he came up with the herd grazing, and in an extraordinary short space of time picked out my two with great glee, and brought them back to me.

Mr. Fripp, the artist of the *Graphic*, was less fortunate than myself, for he lost one and never recovered it. Our animals were a terrible trouble to us in this way, because of those horrible ticks, while I lost one of my best horses with that vile sickness called Red Water. He had been ill for two days, when I found him lying on the ground apparently in awful agony. The veterinary surgeon assured me he could not live, and the officers begged me to shoot him and put him out of his misery.

I went to my tent to fetch my revolver to do so, when someone called out to me, "Never mind, Prior, the poor brute is dead." He must have suffered terribly, for he had pulled up the ground with his teeth and feet, and his mouth was full of earth. I was awfully sorry, for he was my best horse; but oxen as well as horses were dying all round.

I went on to Langhan's Drift, the headquarters of General Newdigate, who received me most kindly. The same evening, I was asked by the officers of the Artillery to dine, and some of them came to fetch me. Having enjoyed a good dinner and a pleasant evening, I started off to return to my tent. But what a trouble I had to find it! It was very dark, and everywhere I went I was being challenged by sentries. At last I spotted my humble abode, which was a peculiar shape, being perfectly square. Everybody was asleep and the camp was quite quiet, but as I advanced a man who was doing sentry-go just in front of my tent challenged me in the ordinary way, "Halt! who goes there?"

"Friend," I replied.

"Advance, friend, and give the countersign."

"I have not got the countersign, sentry; I am not a Zulu."

"I dare say, sir, but I cannot let you pass without the countersign."

"Hang it all, I cannot go back at this time of night and disturb people for it. Can't you see I am a white man?" and I gave him my name; but he was still resolute. At last I whispered, "Look here, sentry, you let me go to my tent and I will give you a little whisky." This was the open *sesame*, and at last I was allowed to go inside. I passed him out a glass very quietly, for I knew I was doing wrong to tempt the man on his beat, although it did seem absurd that, as a white man crossing the camp, I should be challenged as though one of the enemy.

Another night I was lying in my tent, not asleep, when I heard the sentries calling out their numbers round the camp. The first sentry called out "Number one and all's well," then, in a shrill voice, "Number two and all's well," and "Number three is fast asleep." Then immediately, in a gruff voice,

"Number three and all's well, and number four is a d—— liar."

Talking of the artillery reminds me that one day the Rev. G. Smith, the parson who behaved so magnificently at Rorke's Drift when the Zulus attacked it, came over to have a chat with me. I found him a most delightful fellow, one of the quiet but impressive men. I shall have more to say about him later on, but on this occasion, we were chatting outside my tent when we heard that the whole of the artillery horses had stampeded. They were out grazing with the usual guard when something startled them, and they dashed madly into camp, unfortunately making straight for the corner where my little tent was.

As they came on in a dense mass and a cloud of dust, I felt as though the end of the world was upon us, but this brave parson stood on one side and I on the other waving our hands and shouting at them, and by sheer good luck they went by either side of us, knocking over other tents instead of mine, catching in the ropes, and rolling over many of the tent-pegs.

They then made a rush for the lancers' camp, several officers having a very narrow escape; the veterinary surgeon, in his endeavours to stop them, met with a slight accident.

Suddenly the order was given for the feeding bugle to be sounded, and it was the prettiest sight imaginable to see these horses, that had been dashing about wildly, suddenly make for their respective places and actually stand still for their nosebags to be put on; while this was being done, they were easily caught and fastened up.

Hospitality to the correspondents was the rule in camp. I dined with the general and staff and the clergymen: by these latter I mean the Rev. Smith and Father Brindle—the beloved Catholic priest—with the lancers, dragoons, artillery, surgeons, and in fact everybody who had a mess.

My tent in the daytime was looked upon as an artist's studio, and became the rendezvous of all the best fellows in camp during the lazy hours. There was a little cupboard love as well, I think, added to it, for my servant had a wonderful knack of making the most lovely Indian-corn porridge, and very often, instead of the afternoon cup of tea, this stuff went round and the fellows ate it with condensed milk or jam.

Zululand is a rare place for falls; even General Newdigate was laid up for some time owing to a spill from his horse. The fact is, the whole country is studded with ant-hills, and there are any number of ant-bears, notoriously fond of ants, and adopting a method of satisfying their appetite calculated to cause considerable trouble to a rider galloping carelessly across country. The little animal very much resembles a small pig, he has a strong snout and a long tongue, and his method is to dig a hole in the ground a little distance from the ant-hill, and, having burrowed underneath, he inserts his tongue into the tunnel and allows the ants to crawl over and settle on it. As soon as he feels there are a sufficient number collected there to please him, he suddenly withdraws his tongue and swallows the little luxuries.

This process he keeps repeating until he has about finished off the little village or colony residing in each hill. Unfortunately, he does not trouble to fill up the holes again, and the long grass, in most cases falling or being blown across the top of them, you cannot see the danger. Very often, instead of "'Ware wire," it is a case of "'Ware holes."

One morning I was riding with Archibald Forbes down to a collection of huts in search of milk. We heard afterwards it was not always from cows or goats, but we were charged sixpence a bottle, the women settling their share of the money amongst themselves. On this occasion I had my first fall.

We were galloping hard when my horse put both his front legs into one of these ant-bear holes, about two and a half feet deep, and his chest coming up against the opposite side, naturally knocked all the wind out of him, and brought him up so suddenly that I was shot out of my saddle like a stone from a catapult, turning a complete somersault, and landing on the ground

Artist's adventures in Zululand

with my head towards the horse. My helmet was smashed out of all shape, my hand, arms, and legs grazed, and I was shaken to pieces generally.

★★★★★★★★★★★★★★★★

The battlefield of Isandlwana was to be revisited, and General Marshall, who was in command of all the cavalry, was also to command the expeditionary force. It took some little time to organise it, but eventually we started on the 21st of May, exactly four months after the terrible disaster which attended the opening of the war. This expedition from camp grew in size and interest every hour, many wishing in vain to go. I had to obtain express permission from the general, who said he would allow me to join provided I gave him a letter stating that I would take the risk on my own shoulders. This I did, and received the following permission from headquarters, on a slip of blue paper—

Memo.—

Mr. Prior has permission to move with the column to Ingatu and Isandlwana during this week at his own risk.

   (Signed)   E. Newdigate, Maj. Gen.

18.5.79

We left at seven o'clock in the morning, and halted at midday at Robson's Farm, about twelve miles out, and then went on again for Rorke's Drift, which we reached about four in the afternoon, where the column was to bivouac for the night.

By this time, we had been joined by the left wing of the lancers. These with their flying pennons, and the whole of the dragoons with their red coats, made a most picturesque effect as we travelled through the misty valleys and mountainous scenery.

About a mile before we halted, I came across Major Bromhead, who was pleased to see me again, and took me in charge at once, insisting that I should share his room in Fort Melville for the night. We then rode on to where the grand defence had taken place, and he showed me all over it. Certainly, it seemed to me marvellous, considering the position, how that small body of men had been able to resist the onslaught of the Zulus. He then took me down to a new and strong fort that had been built on the banks of the River Buffalo, and introduced me to his brother, one of the heroes of Rorke's Drift.

Next morning, we started at six o'clock, four hundred men of the 24th having joined the column.

At last, the historical hill of Isandlwana came in sight. All glasses were soon out to examine the place, and the wagons were easily seen, still there, not one having been taken away by the enemy. As we got closer, I started on at a gallop, and arrived at the top of the hollow just behind the advance lancers; and then a sight presented itself that it is impossible to describe or to forget.

In all the campaigns I have been in I have not witnessed a scene more horrible. I have seen the dead and dying on a battlefield by hundreds and thousands, but to come suddenly on the spot where the slaughtered battalion of the 24th Regiment and others were lying at Isandlwana was appalling. Here I saw not the bodies, but the skeletons, of men whom I had seen in life and health, some of whom I had known well, mixed up with the skeletons of oxen and horses, with wagons overthrown on their sides, all in the greatest confusion, showing how furious had been the attack of the enemy.

Amidst the various articles belonging to our men, and now scattered over the field of carnage, were letters from wives at home to their husbands in the field, from English fathers and mothers to their sons, portraits of babies and children sent by mothers to the loving fathers—one was signed to "dear darling Dadda"—and other homely little things, remembrances of the dearest associations. I picked up a cigarette-paper book with Coghill's signature in it, also a letter from Mrs. Melville telling her husband how her little boy kept asking when papa was coming home, and then one from his father so full of affection that at last I could not help the tears coming into my eyes when I thought how he was then lying a skeleton above Refugee's Drift. Strangely enough, I found a letter from Lieut. Coghill to Melville, and these two poor fellows were then lying side by side. Well, I saw the most miserable sight I have ever seen, and heard the most piteous tales.

My boy picked up an *assegai* out of a white man's skull; it was in the mouth, and had pinned him to the ground. The second 24th drum was found, and the flag-staff, but alas! the colours were gone—the colours which these grand officers, Coghill and Melville, had so gallantly tried to save.

Skeletons of men lay on the open ground, bleaching under a tropical sun, along miles of country. The individuals could only be recognised by such things as a ring on a finger-bone, a letter or knife, an armlet or neck-chain (which, considered as a fetish, the Zulus would not touch). This identification could only be made with much difficulty, for either the hands of the enemy or the beaks and claws of vultures tearing up the corpses, had, in numberless cases, so mixed up the bones of the dead that the skull of one man, or bones of a leg or arm, now lay with parts of the skeleton of another.

The lancers went about all over the field, often here and there lifting the clothes off the skeletons, or gently pushing them on one side with their lances to see what regiment they belonged to. I almost regretted to see this done, for it seemed like sacrilege, yet it was the wiser course than to run the risk of blood-poisoning by touching the bodies with the hands, and those hands mostly troubled with Natal sores.

All this time scouting parties had been firing the Zulu *kraals* all round, which were blazing brilliantly, while other parties were engaged in hitching the spare horses that had been brought with the column on to some forty wagons and water carts, which were found sufficiently fit to travel, and these having been started off under escort, the return march was commenced, and we returned to Rorke's Drift tired and weary, not only on account of the twenty-five miles of country we had traversed, but by reason of the mournful and melancholy sights we had seen.

During the evening I heard that on the following day there was to be an expedition over the Refugee's Drift where Coghill and Melville had been overtaken by the enemy.

I unfortunately started a little late, and had to hurry along to overtake the column. Arriving at a turn in the road I saw Captain Curling, R.A., halted. He greeted me with, "Hullo, Prior!

Lancers at Isandlwana

not seeing you with the others I turned back to fetch you for fear you should lose the road (just like the good fellow that he was), but now you are here, let us get along quickly," and we proceeded at a full gallop. Just, however, as we were getting up to Colonel Drury Lowe, who commanded the lancers, I had my second fall, for my horse stumbled into another ant-bear hole, this time throwing me over his neck, the impetus being so great that he turned a kind of side somersault and came thumping down on top of me.

Unfortunately, the saddle caught my leg which was under him, and my kneecap was pushed out of joint, his hindquarters resting on my shoulders, and his heels within a few inches of my head. Had he started kicking I should soon have been tucked up, but I heard the colonel say, "Now then men, help Mr. Prior; can't you see he is in trouble?"

I believe I gave a scream as the horse was pulled off me, for my foot was in the stirrup-iron, and as he jumped up and dragged me, I felt the knee-cap slip into its place with a snap. This gave me such agony for a moment that as I lay on the ground, I tore up the long grass by the roots.

I now had lots of assistance, and brandy and rum were poured down my throat.

On hearing the suggestion that I should be sent back to camp, I protested, and begged to be allowed to go on, and was assisted to my horse again. I was determined to see and sketch the grave of poor Coghill and Melville, and to see poor Stewart Smith's skeleton buried; but how I managed to ride the six and a half miles I cannot to this day imagine. To make matters worse, I had to dismount going down the mountain-side, as it was so steep, I could not ride.

I have never been an athlete or an acrobat, but they told me that my hops and jumps on this occasion were a most creditable performance. Wading through the rushing Buffalo River, then up a still steeper hill on the other side was a great undertaking.

It was a most horrible place, and poor Stewart Smith was evidently shot as he was racing down the mountain. Just as he was being buried, I picked up a threepenny-piece, which I handed to

Colonel Harness, R.A. (his late colonel), who was very pleased to have it. I was informed that when Melville and Coghill made the dash to save the colours of the 24th Regiment, Melville unfortunately damaged his knee in getting across the river, and had so much difficulty in climbing the hill on the other side that he begged Coghill to go on and leave him to his fate.

But Coghill stood by him, and succeeded in dragging and helping him almost to the top, within fifty yards of comparative safety, for many of our men were on the top' of the hill with horses and were firing and killing the enemy as they advanced. Both these brave fellows died hard, for a large number of Zulus were found round them. They had chosen a place between two rocks to make their last stand, and died back to back, gallantly trying to save the Queen's Colours.

Our object being accomplished, we started on the return journey. I succeeded in riding my horse back as far as Rorke's Drift. This was about four hours from the time of my fall, but my knee was now swollen to such an extent, and the pain was so intense, that at last I had to be lifted off my horse and left there for the night.

At six the next morning, an ambulance wagon arrived to fetch me, and I was then put into a hospital tent and examined and patched up by the surgeon, Surgeon-Major Brown, who attended the general for an almost similar accident, and, so assiduous was he in fomenting my knee, that at the end of a week, when the column at last started on the road for Ulundi, I was almost able to walk. Fortunately, I had a carriage, and my man rode my horse.

Now General Newdigate was ready to continue the march for Ulundi. Spies had been captured, and been interrogated, communication had been opened with King Cetewayo without any satisfactory result, and the order was out that the column would start in the morning. Landman's Drift was the last point in communication by telegraph with Natal—so when we left it was like saying goodbye. We were still 110 miles from Ulundi, and we could only travel very slowly on account of the ox-wagons, which only covered, at the best, about two and a half miles an hour.

In consequence of my accident, I rode in my cart, and found it tedious to a degree having to go so slowly, but in course of time we arrived at the historical position of Itelezi, where we *laagered*. I say "historical," as it was from here that the Prince Imperial of France started on that memorable reconnoitring expedition which ended so fatally for him. I think I may fairly say that I was the last man he spoke to on leaving camp. It was only a matter of chance, but it occurred in this way.

Our *laager* was formed by heavy wagons, and as I did not wish to get crushed in amongst them, I had my light buggy at one of the corners, and formed up my own little *laager* for myself, so that I could have my horses and men and have a camp of my own. It so happened that I was outside my tent in the morning, when I saw the Prince Imperial on horseback coming from the *laager*, and as he passed me, he said, "Goodbye, Mr. Prior."

"Goodbye, sir. I hope you will have a jolly morning," I replied, as he rode away to join Lieutenant Carey and his escort, which consisted of six white men of Bettington's Horse, six Basutos, and a loyal Zulu guide. The object of this expedition was to survey and make a sketch of the next proposed camping ground.

Having seen him disappear in the distance I returned to my tent to work, but a few hours afterwards I realised that I wanted a good piece of background for the sketch I was engaged on, and, ordering my horse, I started out to ride in search of the correct position. I had not gone very far when I saw General Wood and Colonel Buller riding together, and in the extreme distance I saw a man galloping madly towards them. I was not near enough to hear exactly what took place, but it turned out to be Lieutenant Carey returning from the deplorable disaster which had occurred in the village of Itiotiozi.

I heard afterwards that as he approached, he was stopped by the general and asked, "Where are you coming from?" He was so exhausted, confused, and nervous that he could scarcely speak, but at last he said that they had been attacked by the Zulus when resting in the village and had had to bolt.

He was immediately asked, "Where is the Prince Imperial?"

THE PRINCE IMPERIAL

and holding down his head, with some hesitation he replied he did not know.

No words can express the horror of General Wood and Colonel Buller when they realised that an officer who had gone out on the expedition senior to the prince actually replied that he did not know what had become of him.

He was ordered to report himself to General Newdigate, and rode into camp, the general and the colonel following him.

The news spread like wildfire, and with bated breath everyone was talking of the awful news.

As it was too late for a search party to be sent out that night, orders were given for a strong patrol to go out next morning.

Many of the correspondents were allowed to accompany the little force of cavalry under General Marshall, which was sent to find and recover, if possible, not only the body of the Prince Imperial, but also of the others who had not returned to camp the previous evening.

They were the French correspondent of the Paris *Figaro*, Archibald Forbes of the *Daily News*, Francis Francis of *The Times*, Mackenzie of the *Standard*, Charles Fripp of the *Graphic*, and myself. The search party was spread out over a large area, as it was not known where we might come across the bodies of the unfortunate men. I was riding by the side of Forbes, when, a short distance on our left, we saw one of the troop holding up his rifle and calling out loud. Forbes immediately said, "There it is. Prior. Come on, ride for it!" and a magnificent rider he was.

I followed hard on his heels, and was the fourth man to arrive on the spot. There I saw the Prince Imperial lying on his back, stark-naked, with a thin gold chain round his neck, to which was attached a locket containing the portrait of his father, the late Emperor Napoleon the Third. The Zulus had stripped him, and taken away every particle of clothing, but, looking upon this gold chain and locket as a fetish, had respected it, and left it still round his neck.

The French correspondent, leaning over with tears streaming down his face, took an English penny from his pocket and placed it over the prince's eye (the one which had received a spear-thrust) in the hopes of closing it.

On carefully examining the body it was found that he had been stabbed twenty-one times, and the bodies of the two troopers of Bettington's Horse were found at only a few yards distance, also covered with *assegai* wounds.

Whilst we gathered round the corpse, vedettes had been posted round the spot for some distance, in case Zulus might be lurking round, and having recovered from the momentary shock and horror of the situation, a stretcher was formed of blankets laid upon lancers' spears, and the body having been placed upon it, the stretcher was carried to the ambulance wagon, which had been brought out for that purpose, by General Marshall, Colonel Drury Lowe, Major Stewart, and several officers of the 17th Lancers. A procession was then formed, which solemnly marched into camp.

The corpse was next day sent down to Natal and thence to England.

I went to General Newdigate and told him that I wanted to work all night, and asked permission to have a light in my tent. I assured him that I would cover it round with a blanket and that it should not be seen outside in the smallest degree. He informed me that it was against the rules of the camp, but that under the circumstances, and on this special occasion, he would grant me the permission, and an order was written so that the sentry near my tent should not interfere with me.

Once alone I lighted my lamp and sat down and pitched into work, and by five o'clock in the morning I had made nine sketches in connection with the Prince Imperial's untimely end.

My best horse was saddled, and my man, with my sketches in the regulation red envelope of the office, was only waiting for daylight to start and gallop to Landman's Drift to save the post, which he succeeded in doing, and my sketches were the only ones that appeared in London in connection with that sad event.

★★★★★★★★★★★★★★★

There are no doubt many reasons that may be advanced for the unfortunate scene which I am about to relate. The disaster at Isandlwana, as well as the many occasions on which the

The passage of the Prince Imperial's body

Zulus had given us a bad time, had no doubt had its effect on the minds of the men. Then, too, the darkness at night was very dense. How often have I, as well as others, on a pitch-dark night, imagined I could see all sorts of things moving. A tiny bush, a stump of a low palm, by steadfastly gazing at them, I could swear they were advancing on me.

At last, the nerves would be worked up to such a state, that a falling leaf or twig would be sufficient to turn doubt into certainty. In the present instance the rifle was clutched tight, pointed at the object, and in sheer desperation was fired by one of our pickets. That was enough, however regrettable, to startle the whole camp.

I was in my tent working in Zangweni camp when I heard a distant shot from our pickets, followed by another, and then two more. Instantly there was a commotion in our *laager* as everyone rushed off to the tents to obtain firearms or came out of them ready for eventualities, and then a volley from the picket's supports was distinctly heard. At the same moment our alarm bugle sounded, the tents were struck, that is to say pulled down, and we all rushed to take up our position by the wagons. My boy gave me my helmet, greatcoat, and revolver, and then down came my tent.

Suddenly some of our officers imagined they could see a black mass approaching, and gave word to fire, and instantly a most terrific fire was going on all round the *laager*. For some ten minutes or so the most deafening noise of musketry was kept up; horses got loose and careered about amongst us. Our native allies appeared almost mad with fear, and the danger we ran of being shot by our men was horrible; as it was, five of our men were wounded by our own fire.

I went up to the edge of the *laager*, and looking over a wagon tried to see if I could catch sight of the enemy, and as I turned round, I saw any number of our native allies with their muskets pointing straight towards me.

I need scarcely say I soon cleared out of that position. The brutes were firing all over the camp, and I could hear the bullets whiz through the air, from one point of the *laager* to the other. A more disgraceful scene I have never witnessed, more particularly when we realised that six rounds of canister were actually fired by the artillery, without having seen one single enemy. There was one redeeming feature in the whole affair, and that was that the pickets fell back and came into camp in Indian file, as steadily as on parade, although under a terrible fire from our own square. The bugle sounded the "Cease fire," but we kept under arms all night. It was a fine sight to see the pickets march out again to take up their original positions.

★★★★★★★★★★★★★★★★

When only a few marches from Ulundi, an order was issued that no private cart or carriage would be allowed to proceed beyond a certain point, and sure enough when we arrived there sentries had been so placed as to form what is known as "camp gates," through which everything had to pass.

Just before arriving at this position, I saw one of the correspondent's carts being refused permission to go on. Suddenly an idea struck me. Lord Chelmsford was close by, so, approaching and saluting him in the most approved fashion, I asked him if he had any objection to my cart going forward. "You see, sir, I have my sketching materials and paper; besides, my bad knee compels me to ride in my carriage a good deal, and I shall never get on without it."

"Well, Mr. Prior," he said, with a smile, "I have no objection, but I am not in command of this division; you must apply to General Newdigate—there he is, just over to your right."

"Oh, thank you, My Lord," and I hastened over to him.

"Excuse me, General Newdigate, for troubling you, but do you mind my cart going forward? Lord Chelmsford says he has no objection if you have not." I said this all in one breath, and the general looked steadily at me and said, "Well, Mr. Prior, if Lord Chelmsford, who is commander-in-chief, has no objection, of course I cannot have."

"Then, sir, might I ask you to write on my card to let my cart pass?"

I shall never forget my feelings of gratitude, as well as delight, when he most kindly wrote on my paste-board:

Let Mr. Prior's cart pass. (Signed) E. A. Newdigate.

And as I rode on to see it go through the gates, my heart was thumping almost to bursting-point with pleasure, for now I should still have my tent and little comforts with me; once through those terrible gates, I knew I was all right.

The other men with private carts were very jealous, but also very generous, and did not complain. If they had, there was just the possibility that my permission might have been revoked.

Very shortly after this incident I came up with Surgeon-Major Brown—the surgeon who had attended to my poor knee. He looked remarkably hot. I called out to him, "Hullo, major, you look jolly warm."

He said "Right you are; it's a regular swelterer today."

"How about a brandy-and-soda, major; or would you prefer whisky?"

"Now, Prior, I don't like chaff on these occasions; presently you will ask me if I like it iced."

"I don't know about ice, but I can give you a cool drink. Let us bear away a little to the left and get up to my cart, and we will both have one."

I don't think I ever saw a man's face and eyes glisten with greater pleasure when he realised that I was not chaffing.

"Now then, John," I said to my servant, "get me out a couple of sodas, and be sharp about it!" and very soon we drank each other's health as though we had been in a club in Durban. I could not help smiling when I thought if Lord Chelmsford had seen us, he would not have thought it so very strange that I wanted my cart to go on to carry my sketching materials.

When we were encamped at Upoka River, three clergymen joined us after a most perilous journey. On leaving Landman's Drift they were told that the post, in charge of Basutos, was just ahead of them, and that they could easily catch them up and then all travel together. This they tried to do, but unfortunately Basutos are splendid riders and were travelling quickly.

These clergymen could discern them in the extreme distance, but failed to come up with them. The road being very rough at this point, and night coming on very quickly, they decided to bivouac and pass the night in a mealie field and wait for daylight.

They knee-haltered their horses, and then actually went to sleep. When they told us of this, and described the hills, the *kraals* they saw, and the river, we realised it was the exact spot where the Prince Imperial was killed.

Zulus had been seen by the Basuto post here, and how these three men escaped with their lives and arrived in camp safely is a marvel.

Talking of clergymen reminds me of a conversation I had with the Rev. G. Smith. We were riding together one morning, when he asked me, "Why do you carry a revolver. Prior?"

"Well," I said, "for a very good reason. If I unfortunately get into a tight corner, I intend five shots for the enemy and the last one for myself, for I am never going to be taken alive by a Zulu."

"Oh, do you think that very brave?" he smilingly asked in reply. "Do you really mean that? Would you really wantonly and with premeditation take that life which had been given you? Would it not be better to suffer a little agony, that you might have to bear if you fell into the hands of the enemy, than to take the life which God gave you?"

I had never looked at it in that light before, but so much was I impressed with his seriousness and the nice way in which he put the matter, that I in turn looked at him and said, "Smith, you are right, and I promise you that I will never take my own life."

He changed this conversation by telling me a little incident that had occurred to him during the fight at Rorke's Drift.

"I was going about," he said, "encouraging the men and handing out packets of cartridges to them, when I heard a Tommy, who was blazing away, using the most dreadful language, and as I gave him cartridges, I touched him on the shoulder and said, 'My man, can't you fight without swearing? Think of your God Almighty.'"

"'Yes, sir, that's all right, but this is my God Almighty at present,' as he raised his rifle to his shoulder and fired."

It was at this camp that Cetewayo's *indunas* arrived with a message offering peace if we would return to Natal. Lord Chelmsford sent them back with his answer to the king, and they were to return again on a certain day, and as that day arrived it was quite evident that the general was very anxious, and he, with General Newdigate and General Marshall were looking over the edge of the *laager* anxiously, in hopes of catching sight of the king's messengers.

The night that the ambassadors were expected back was the darkest one I ever remember. It was almost impossible to see anything without a lantern, and this, of course we were not allowed to have. The going was pretty bad from one tent to another, but when one realises that all the oxen and horses were inside the *laager*, one may very easily understand how very unpleasant it was. With hundreds of horses very often carelessly tethered to a peg, it is not strange that some would get loose during the night and stroll about amongst the tents, sometimes falling over the ropes; one actually did fall on a tent full of men and nearly suffocated some of them.

The staff at last issued a notice that if any of the horses got loose and came down near headquarter tents, they would be branded. Funnily enough one of the staff surgeon's horses did, and in the morning, it was found going about camp with a large "V.R." and "P.O." branded on it, meaning it belonged to the Queen's Post Office. This brand would never come out.

We correspondents did our utmost to prevent our horses getting loose, but Francis Francis of the *Times* was unlucky, and we discovered one of his horses with a broad arrow nine inches long on one side, and on the other a "Crown," a "V.R.," and a large "P.O." So poor Francis had to ride about as though he had been enrolled into Her Majesty's Postal Service as a postman.

I was not at all surprised at the order, for it is certainly most disagreeable to have horses strolling about camp.

★★★★★★★★★★★★★★

At last, after many weeks of hard marching, we arrived on the banks of the White Umvolozi, where a large *laager* was formed of the wagons in a square formation; the oxen and horses were sent out to graze, with strong guards to see that they did not roam too far.

Ulundi (the capital *kraal*, or town, of King Cetewayo) was to be seen in the distance, and speculation was rife as to whether the enemy was going to fight or not.

Colonel Buller was ordered to reconnoitre the enemy's ground, and with Lord William Beresford and Sir Thomas Hesketh acting as *aides-de-camp*, crossed the White Umvolozi with five hundred mounted men, and made what might be called an interesting and exciting reconnaissance.

The force was divided into two columns. They soon came up with some of the enemy, whom they pursued; but these were evidently acting as decoy ducks, for as Colonel Buller at the head of three hundred men chased them, and approached a *donga*. Sir Thomas Hesketh descried a large number of the enemy. Upon this the order was given to wheel about, for the object of this reconnaissance was not to engage the enemy so much as to find out a good position where Lord Chelmsford could teach them a lesson, which he did on the following day.

On seeing our men fall back, the Zulus fired a tremendous volley into them, bringing four men out of their saddles.

It was quite evident that the old trick, which they so successfully played at Hlobane and other places, was again attempted by our wily enemy, and that but for the sharp look-out kept. Colonel Buller would have been entrapped by them.

The object for which they went out being satisfactory, a retreat was ordered under a heavy fire from the enemy. It was during this time that Lord William Beresford rode at a Zulu and ran his sword through his shield as well as the Zulu.

In the retreat Lord William Beresford, turning round, saw the four legs of a white horse kicking in the air, and realising at once that it belonged to one of our men, rode straight for it, to discover that his surmise was quite right, the horse had been shot and the man had fallen half-stunned.

"Get up!" he said to the man, and he seemed too dazed to answer; whereupon Lord William said, "If you don't get up at once I will jump down and punch your head," at which the man did rise, and at last Lord William succeeded in helping him on to the horse behind him, the man clutching Beresford round the waist, and so they galloped off.

All the time this was taking place the Zulus were firing all they knew from a *donga* close by; but I am happy to say that both got away safely. If any man ever won a V.C. Lord William certainly did on that occasion, and eventually he received it.

I remember when he came up to us that his back was one mass of blood. We all thought the man was wounded, but on close inspection we found that he had only damaged his nose in the fall from his horse.

As the cavalry returned from this reconnaissance, they had to recross the White Umvolozi at a drift between two hills. Some Zulus had already occupied the position and were potting away at them as they crossed, while our infantry and artillery on our side pounded away at the enemy to prevent them, if possible, from coming down to closer quarters.

Those who watched the brave little band return, declared that it was touch and go whether they would get across safely. However, they succeeded in doing so, and just as Colonel Buller was going to return to camp to report to the general the result of his reconnaissance, someone informed him that a man was left behind, and turning round and looking through his glasses he did discover someone calmly standing on the enemy's side of the river sketching.

He called out to him to come back immediately—an order to which at first no attention was paid. Buller once more called out, ordering him to come across at once, or he would have him fetched and sent as a prisoner to the rear. This energetic little man, who had been sketching, turned out to be Charlie Fripp, of the *Graphic*, who had been making notes and sketches of the background for his drawing of the retreat of the cavalry, and he was most indignant at having been ordered about by anyone.

Fripp came up to us, he was fairly foaming with rage. "The idea of being insulted and told I should be sent to the rear as a prisoner!" Then seeing Lord William Beresford, he rode over to him, and demanded to know who the man was who had spoken to him in that insulting manner, to which Lord William, who was still smothered in the blood of the man whose life he had saved, replied, "You know Mr. Fripp, quite well without my telling you."

"I don't," replied Fripp, "and I desire to know who it was."

Unfortunately, he spoke in such an offensive manner that at last Lord William said in a quiet sort of way, "If you don't speak more politely, I'll pull you off your horse and thrash you."

This was quite enough for Fripp, who was a plucky little devil, and without more ado he jumped off his horse and squared up to Lord William, and was going for him in rare style, when, in self-defence, Beresford had to show fight. It was quite exciting for the moment that it lasted, and Fripp certainly showed that he could use his fists, but Lord William who was a notorious bruiser and an all-round sportsman, did not want to hurt him, but with a straight one from the shoulder pushed rather than knocked him down.

Fripp was so excited and in such a rage that he "up with his foot" and kicked Lord William, whereupon it was most amusing to see the latter dance round roaring with laughter and saying, "Oh, he's kicked me! Take him away; I'm frightened. He's kicked me!"

In another moment Archie Forbes and myself had caught hold of Fripp, who fought like a perfect little demon, and we tore his coat almost to pieces before we could get the best of him and haul him away to his tent.

It was certainly one of the most amusing incidents I remember out in those parts.

★★★★★★★★★★★★★★★★

While our natives and servants were at the river getting water, the Zulus from a hillock on the opposite side would sometimes treat us to a pot-shot; but we had a couple of guns on our side, and we would give them around of shell, shrapnel, or canister the moment any of them appeared. They used, however, to shriek out a number of defiant terms to us, saying we were a set of cowards and all very well behind a *laager*, but did not dare to go and meet them in the open, and that if we did, they would annihilate us.

As the evening came on, we saw a black column of Zulus streaming out of Ulundi and coming straight towards us.

We heard afterwards that the witchdoctors had chosen out a few of their enemies, had tortured and killed them, and then smeared their blood on the lips of the warriors. Very often the heart would be cut out of the victim, divided into little pieces and given to the warriors to eat, and they had humbugged the fighting men into the belief that our bullets would be utterly harmless against them. The king then reviewed his army and told it to go out, kill and eat the white devils.

The black mass that we saw advancing was the centre column, composed of those famous fighting regiments that had been a terror to every other tribe in that part of Africa.

They had been worked up with the aid of native beer, to the height of fighting madness and enthusiasm, and now came on with the full intention of wiping us out of existence—very kind of them! Fortunately for us it turned out somewhat differently.

The chanting of their weird, wild, war-songs, and shouts of defiance coming over the hills and through the trees in the gloaming had a distinctly disagreeable effect, but as darkness came on it was even more irritating to the nerves—it was nasty. I was walking up and down outside the *laager* with Archie Forbes, and trying to speak, but I found I could not. I even shook and my teeth chattered, perhaps you will say with fright—possibly it was so.

While watching the movements of this column we noticed two more immense black masses of Zulus coming on, one diverging to the left, the other to the right. These were the horns of the enemy, marching evidently with the intention of surrounding us. There was very little doubt left now that we were in for a big fight on the morrow.

Our *laager* was as large as the wagons placed close to each other would allow, but it was a pretty tight fit when all the cattle and horses were driven in, and there was not too much room for the headquarter staff and those others who had to be inside.

Very shortly after the animals had been brought in a very curious commotion occurred amongst them. How it happened no one seemed to know. The animals no doubt took fright at something, for they started moving in a circle, quietly enough at first, but gradually increasing the pace until at last it became a mad rush, and the more we tried to stop them with the waving of hands and shouts the worse and madder they seemed to become. The animals' snortings and bellowings, and the awful dust they made rolling in clouds above them, turned the whole scene into a perfect pandemonium.

This awful stampede eventually wore itself out, but we all thought it was a most lucky thing the Zulus did not charge us at the same time, as the two episodes together might have been mighty unpleasant.

This disturbance was no sooner over than we had a much worse excitement and alarm, which proved to be quite a serious one.

It appeared that when the *laager* was formed trenches were dug all round some little distance in front of each face, in which the white troops were to pass the night, so as to be ready in case of an attack, and then still further out other trenches were made in which our native allies were to keep watch. Everything seemed to be in perfect order. I had just had my scratch sort of dinner, and was preparing to lie down under my cart, which was very snugly wedged in between two wagons, when I heard a shot fired, and then another, and in a few moments a kind of whirlwind seemed to be coming towards us, which proved to be the native and white troops all mixed together dashing for the *laager*. Some clambered over the wagons, while others crawled underneath, in their mad endeavour and haste to get inside.

Under the wagon next to mine was General Sir Evelyn Wood, and in the mad rush of the troops he was rolled over and over, and his head coming in contact with the wheel of a wagon, was badly cut, and had to be surgically treated.

On investigation it turned out that one of the natives had seen what he thought to be an enemy lurking in the grass, and fired at him, and the rest of the natives, under the impression that the enemy was charging them, jumped up and fell back on the white troops; these in turn finding these naked devils right in amongst them, thought they were Zulus, and jumped up and also dashed for the *laager*.

It was certainly much to be regretted, but still more so that two hundred men of a certain regiment, which shall be nameless, actually left their rifles in the trench in their haste to get into camp. Had it been a genuine Zulu charge the whole affair might undoubtedly have turned out a disaster; as it was, the men were soon got in hand again, and returned to their posts. This time, I believe, the disposition of the troops was changed.

No further incident of importance took place that night, and we all slept in our clothes as well as we could under the circumstances, remembering that tomorrow was the test of arms—white versus black.

At daybreak the troops were drawn up in formation, and waiting for the order to advance. Buller's Horse crossed the river above and below our front, and found the country abandoned. Then the order was given for the whole force to go forward. As soon as we had crossed a drift, got clear of the bush, and arrived in the open, the troops were formed into a great square, with artillery, engineers, hospital corps, natives, &c., in the centre, the 17th Lancers bringing up the rear. We were then marched in the direction of Ulundi, and halted on the exact spot selected by Buller the day before, as a good fighting ground.

It appeared afterwards that King Cetewayo had also instructed his army to draw us on to it, so there was nothing to complain about on either side, for both had chosen the same position to try conclusions. Buller's Horse, on ahead, soon came in contact with the enemy, and opened the ball, and drew them on by steadily retreating fighting, until the Zulus, showing up very strong and determinedly on all sides, compelled him to canter back into the square, and thus enable the infantry to become engaged. On came the enemy the great fight commenced in earnest, and for the three-quarters of an hour that it lasted was as disagreeable as one could wish for.

The air seemed alive with the whistling of bullets and slugs and pieces of cooking-pot legs fired from elephant guns as they came banging in amongst us from all directions.

Our artillery practice was very fine, but it failed to daunt the Zulus. The rockets must have astonished them a good deal, for

THE ZULU WAR: THE BATTLE OF ULUNDI. INSIDE THE SQUARE.

they did us. I saw one fired, and watched its triumphal progress amongst the enemy, until, catching a corner of a hut, it suddenly altered its direction, then, striking the ground, it once more deviated from its proper course, and came straight back at us, luckily missing our square by a quarter of a yard. My faith in rockets and tubes has considerably weakened since that occasion.

All those who were not actually engaged in fighting were ordered to keep as low down as possible, and I was doing so kneeling, when I discovered the Rev. Gore, who was Principal Chaplain to the Forces, was by my side. "It's very warm, Prior," he said.

To which I readily agreed, as a bullet banged into one of our native allies close to us and rolled him over. By the way, it was very funny to see these men lying flat on the ground, with their shields covering their backs.

Another bullet killed a horse behind us and made him jump at least three feet in the air. Then all at once there appeared to be a perfect hailstorm of bullets in our direction, and we both wriggled on our knees, until one in particular passed between us with a nasty "*phew*," and my friend exclaimed, "My God, Prior, that was close."

This sort of thing went on all the time, until I heard the Zulus were said to be preparing to rush one of our corners.

Hastily asking one of the 2nd Dragoon Guards to hold my horse for a moment, I ran down to where the 21st and 58th Regiments were heavily engaged with some Zulus, said to be 6,000 strong and 30 deep, who were charging, and it was then that I heard Lord Chelmsford say to the troops, "Men, fire faster; can't you fire faster?" Now it is not my business to question the wisdom of this remark, but I cannot help contrasting it with Lord Wolseley's well-known order, "Fire slow, fire slow!"

However, the Zulus who charged this corner did not succeed in breaking it; the terrific fire of our men made them stagger, halt, and fall back a straggling mass, leaving a heap of dead and dying on the ground.

I have read since various statements as to how near the enemy got to our square, and it often stated that twenty to thirty paces was the closest, but I can say that I personally went out and reached the nearest one in nine paces, so their onslaught was pretty determined.

This charge and its failure seemed to decide the fate of Ulundi, for there was a mighty cheer as the enemy gave way, and the square opened to let out the lancers and Buller's Horse, who burst like an avalanche on the broken enemy, the cavalry most thoroughly upholding its reputation for dash and daring not, unfortunately, without loss. Captain Wyatt Edgell was killed and two officers wounded, and there were many fatalities amongst the men. Many most interesting duels—sword versus spear—took place, in all cases to the advantage of the sword, although in some cases not without damage to the swordsman.

While watching this exciting charge, I put my hand in my pocket for my sketch-book, when I suddenly remembered I had left it in the holster of my saddle. I often used to carry it there, so as to have it ready at a moment's notice, which in this case was just about as stupid as a cavalryman having his sword fixed to his saddle as, if thrown and attacked by an enemy, he has naturally lost possession of his sword.

Bushing back to my horse, which was still being held by a trooper of the 2nd Dragoons, I noticed the flap of my holster was unfastened, and putting my hand inside I discovered, to my horror, it was not there. I felt again in my pockets, in my saddle-bags, and my haversack, I searched on the ground; no, it was not there. The trooper said he knew nothing about it.

Now I had only been using it a short time before I ran down to the corer, so what could have become of it? The more I thought, the more horrified I seemed to become at the awful loss, and at last I stood as though petrified. My sketchbook, containing all the notes I had made in the campaign and sketches of this battle, was gone, and in sheer despair I fell on the ground and burst into tears.

General Newdigate at that moment came by, and in his kindly way asked me what was the matter, but I was almost too miserable to be able to explain. At last, I did so, and he patted me on the shoulder and told me to cheer up. At the same moment Sir

William Gordon Gumming, who was by my side, said, "Never mind, Prior, here is my sketch-book; get up and run about, and make more sketches of costumes and background, and I will guarantee you will get out of your troubles."

This kindly thought and suggestion had this effect: I took the advice given, and soon obtained enough detail for my purposes. But what about my sketch-book? I offered twenty-five pounds for it in regimental orders, but I never saw it again.

Later on in my life I met a man who said he knew all about it, and actually knew the man who had it, but he had given his word of honour to keep the secret, and he would not break it. He said the man who had it was too ashamed to return it. I said, "Nonsense, he could have posted it without any name."

I felt such contempt for any man who would lend himself to such contemptible tricks that I never spoke to this one again. All worry, however, with regard to my book was soon dissipated, for by this time I had wandered up to the corner of the square, facing Ulundi, when I heard the deep voice of Forbes as he called out, "Come on. Prior, for Ulundi; ride for it, old chap!" and digging spurs into my horse it soon became a race between literature and art.

He was a great rider, and well mounted, and he beat me by a neck.

At the entrance of the king's *kraal*, which was already in flames, we met Lord William Beresford, who had been the first to arrive in the *kraal*, and was nicknamed "Ulundi Beresford" in consequence. The capital of Zululand, in which many a horrible and ghastly deed of fetishism had been perpetrated, was indeed a very large village, and at the corner we had made for stood the king's palace, burning furiously.

Mr. Drummond had joined us, and it was suggested that we should go inside and have a look at Cetewayo's palace.

At the entrance we saw several large baskets of Mabal corn, of which horses and cattle generally were exceedingly fond; it was a kind of millet which the natives ground into flour for porridge; and here we left our horses to enjoy themselves, while we entered on foot.

Having gone through a gateway, we found ourselves in a large courtyard, at the opposite end of which was a large door leading into another courtyard, then another door and another courtyard.

Having traversed these three, we found ourselves fairly in amongst the flames of the king's palace, and while the others proceeded to one corner, I ran down a long passage to the right to obtain a sketch.

I had flames on three sides of me, but I cared not. I was so delighted to be able to obtain a drawing of this savage king's residence, that I only thought of the work, and did not know that Forbes and Beresford had left me to it.

I may have been some four or five minutes sketching, when I saw some black object pop up above the palisade on my left. What can it be? I thought to myself, and clambering up, I actually saw a real live Zulu, with spears and shield. Then I suddenly took in the situation: I was alone with fire on three sides of me and the Zulu running to get round the courtyards, so as, if possible, to cut off my retreat.

With sketch-book in one hand and pencil in the other, I started on a run for my life. Great Scot! how I ran to try and get out of this frightful trap.

As I tore through the first courtyard, I saw no one, and through the second I saw no one, but as I entered the third and turned my head, I saw the Zulu turn the corner of the first courtyard, racing for me as hard as he could.

My God, I thought, I am lost! The fact that I had a revolver by my side, and might have made a stand, never entered my head. I simply ran for dear life, and as I emerged into the open, by everything that is holy, there was my horse still eating out of the basket.

Springing on his back, and digging my spurs in, he made a wild leap forward, and as I dug my spurs more and more into him, so he went for all he was worth. I had not bothered about gathering up reins, but simply guided him by pulling his head round by the mane and his ears. In his wild career he put his feet in the reins and tore them asunder, fortunately without stum-

CETSHEWAYO

bling or throwing me, for this would have meant the end of the rider.

I had had a shock, for, in the first place, I did not know Forbes and the others had left me alone, and, secondly, I never thought for a moment that any Zulu was hardy enough to remain in the *kraal*, knowing we were destroying it, so I may perhaps be excused if I say I continued my mad gallop until I came up with our troops once more.

Meeting Sir William Gordon Cumming, I told him of my little escapade, when he replied, "By Jove! I wonder where Forbes and Beresford are? Let us return and see if we can find them, and go for that Zulu," and to my utter astonishment I started back with him full of pluck and fight.

We did not enter the *kraal* at the same point, but skirted round it. Presently we came across a jolly nice hut, and Cummings said, "There ought to be something in this place," and he crawled in while I held his horse, and he came out with some nice spears and curiosities. At the next hut I went in, and while there I heard him calling, "Come out of that Prior; we had better get away. There have been three or four bullets pass me; there are evidently a lot of Zulus still about."

So, we had to give up our search and quietly return to the square without having seen any of my three former companions.

The order was then given for the square to return to our *laager*, and on the road, I met Forbes and Lord Beresford, who told me that they had got separated in the burning *kraal* from Drummond, and they had not seen him since, and I regret to say that he evidently fell a victim to a Zulu spear or gun, for he was never seen again.

Safe in the *laager*, I was chatting with a commissariat officer when a captain who had been on picket duty outside Ulundi came in. Turning to me he said, "You had a lucky escape this morning."

"Yes," I said, "a Zulu chased me."

"There were five," he said, "for I saw them, and I thought that they would have you, but you were too nippy in getting on to your pony. They threw several *assegais* at you, but luckily missed you. I was too far off to be of any use, and my troopers could not get to you in time, but by Jove, you did get away smartly!"

It appeared in explanation later on that Forbes thought I had gone further into Ulundi, and returned for his horse, and told my servant, who was holding him, to follow him and bring my animal along with him, and he would pick me up at the other end of the *kraal*. But my man said, "No, sir, my master left his horse here and will come back and expect to find it;" but Forbes felt so sure that I had left that he made my man follow him to go in search of me.

Great Heavens! how lucky it was that my good man George left my pony eating that Mobala corn.

I was chatting with some men about the fight and the day's work, when Forbes called me on one side to tell me he was going to ride down country for Durban as hard as he could, and was going to start almost immediately. If I had a sketch of the fight ready, he would take it with him and post it for me, and it would be the first in London.

Getting hold of a large sheet of paper from my cart, I threw myself on the ground, and in half an hour had a rough sketch ready. Forbes's great ride is so well known, even in these days, that it is not necessary for me to relate it. His object was that his account should be the first to reach England, and, going over to the general, he had offered to carry information of the success of the battle round *via* Durban to General Crealock, who was then still marching on the coast route.

Lord Chelmsford readily accepted the offer, and furnished him with a fresh horse and an escort of six Lancers, thus turning Forbes into a despatch-rider with all the attendant privileges. As he left, I and a few others gave him a cheer and a Godspeed, and away he went on his memorable ride, which was a distinctly risky one for the first eight or ten miles, but after that it was comparatively easy going. Posts and forts had been established every ten or fifteen miles by our column as we advanced, and at each of these, as Forbes arrived, he was furnished with a fresh horse and escort of six men, and a jolly good meal and drink. This went on until he arrived at Landman's Drift. Then he continued alone to Ladysmith, where he obtained the loan of a buggy and pair of horses, with a promise that he would pay £100 if he damaged either.

Arrived in Maritzburg, he took post cart and rail for Durban, where he arrived in record time, very much done up. But he telegraphed his account and posted my sketch, which arrived and was published in the *Illustrated London News* a clear week ahead of any other.

The battle took place on the morning of Friday, June 4th, Forbes leaving in the afternoon; and no sooner had he departed than I made up my mind I would rush down country as fast as possible and make my sketches of all I had seen in the last few days quietly in Durban, and if possible, take them with me in the next steamer for England. I left on the following morning. My horses having had a long rest and good feeding, were in great fettle, and we travelled along at quite a good pace, and everything on the road went merrily.

Unfortunately, on one or two occasions I made bad calculations about distances, and got benighted twice. On the second occasion it was particularly unfortunate, as night was fast falling, and I knew by the contour of the country that I was close to where the Prince Imperial was killed.

I was going along thinking of that horrible catastrophe, when I suddenly realised that I was off the road, and on consultation with my man he informed me that the horses were also rather done up. It was so dark that I could not see the road, and I was unwilling to strike a light for fear of attracting attention from any lurking Zulu who might be about, for this spot seemed to strike terror into me. I dismounted and felt with my feet as well as my hands for some distance to the left, and then went over to the right of the cart. Suddenly coming up with some deep ruts, I knew I had struck the road again as a bit of good luck. I then whispered to my man to take one of the horses out of the cart and ride on with me to the next post.

"No," he said, "you go on, sir, and I will bring the cart on later."

"Not a bit of it, George. You do as I tell you. You have no

revolver, and if by any chance we are attacked at this miserable spot, I am going to stand by you."

"Never mind, sir," he continued, "you go on and I will bring the cart in."

This indomitable pluck shamed me, and I said, "Very well, then, let the horse rest, and we will go in half an hour," and as good luck would have it, the horses seemed to muster up fresh pluck, as though they felt there was a good feed waiting for them at the camp, and then we started off again quite gaily.

Even then, however, I did not reach the post at Itelezi until one o'clock in the morning, and was more than delighted when I heard the challenge of the sentry, for every now and then I imagined I could see what I thought was the form of a man advancing on us, and I tried to pierce the darkness in search of possible danger.

On arriving at camp, we found two of the officers had been sitting up rather late playing cards. Hearing me arrive, they turned out to welcome me, and supper, a good drink, and a comfortable bed soon made me forget the troubles of the last few hours.

Bill Beresford and His Victoria Cross

By Archibald Forbes

Some fifteen years ago the prevailing opinion regarding the brothers Beresford—Lord Charles and Lord William—probably was that they were both more or less crazy. Their father, the fourth Marquis of Waterford, was a clergyman. It is not alleged that this circumstance contributed to intensify the impression; and in point of fact the clerical marquis was a sedate well-ordered divine, who was a dean, and no doubt might have been a bishop had he aspired to that dignity.

But their uncle, the third Lord Waterford, had earned by sedulous exertion the popular appellation of "the mad marquis." He rode his horse over toll-gates by lantern light, distinguished himself in miscellaneous pugilistic encounters, made and won the wildest wagers, and finally broke his neck in the hunting-field.

It was supposed that the spirit of this ancestor had revived in his madcap nephews. Lord Charles—far better known as "Charlie"—was a midshipman who appeared to live for larks. Lord William—whom all his world knew as "Bill"—was a lieutenant in a lancer regiment who in the hunting-field and in steeple-chase riding had broken pretty well every bone in his body, and some of them several times over. Men who knew the brothers well realised that behind their madcap daring and their wild recklessness lay a capacity for earnest work when the opportunity should offer. It should be said that their eccentricities were never sullied by taint of anything gross or dishonourable; it lay in no man's mouth to say that a Beresford ever did a coarse, a

ARCHIBALD FORBES

shabby, or an ungenerous thing.

People had grown to comprehend that Charles Beresford was something other than a merry-andrew, before that critical moment of the bombardment of Alexandria, when he laid his little *Condor* right under the guns of a hostile battery, and not less by skill than by daring contributed materially to the successful issue. Since then, he has served as a Minister of the Crown, and when until lately he spoke from his place in Parliament, he was listened to as a leading practical authority on naval reforms.

William has three medals for as many campaigns; has won the Victoria Cross by the deed of splendid valour I am about to narrate; was the sole and most efficient staff officer to a brigade composed of uniquely heterogeneous elements out of which good work could be got only by a rare combination of tact, firmness, and veritable leadership; and is now fulfilling adequately the important duties of Military Secretary to the Viceroy of India. Under these circumstances people have now for some time left off regarding the brothers Beresford as crazy.

Lord Charles I only know; Bill—I won't call him Lord William any more—has been my comrade *per mare et terras* for more years than either he or I care to reckon. I met him first on a night march in the autumn manoeuvres on Salisbury Plain, in August 1872. He was then a "galloper" to the general commanding the cavalry brigade. General and brigade had lost their way in the darkness, and Bill got the order to go and find it. He was riding a violent cross-grained mare, which resented being forced to leave the other horses.

I gave him a lead for a little way. As I turned, his mare reared straight on end; I knew it, dark as it was, because her forefoot touched my shoulder. Then there was a thud on the short thick grass carpeting the chalk of the great plain. The brute had "come over" on Bill. There was a groan, but it was from the mare as she fell heavily, not from her rider. He was out from under her somehow before she began to struggle, was in the saddle as she scrambled to her feet, gave her the spur, and forced the cowed brute at a gallop out into the darkness.

Bill and I went up the gruesome Khyber Pass together, in

November 1878, with the little army which gallant one-armed old Sir Sam Browne led to the invasion of Afghanistan. Across the narrowest gut of that gloomy defile, perched high on its isolated rock, stands the fortress of Ali Musjid, held against us by a strong Afghan garrison. Ali Musjid was the impediment which had to be subdued before we could penetrate farther into the bowels of the Afghan land. Two long broken ridges reach up to the base of the Ali Musjid rock, separated from each other by the valley down the centre of which flows, or rather rushes, the Khyber stream.

At the head of one brigade Sir Sam himself moved on the fortress along the rugged right-hand ridge; the other brigade, commanded by General Appleyard, had its route along the left-hand upland.

Rather late in the day, when the force was fully committed to this movement, it became apparent that because of the intervening ravine, quick intercommunication with Appleyard was rendered difficult. The Afghans in the fort were no fools; they had recognised the existence of the interval between the two brigades; and they did their level best to keep the force bisected by pouring a steady stream of artillery and musketry down the valley.

Sir Sam wanted to send a message to Appleyard. Beresford, who was then an *aide-de-camp* to the Viceroy of India, and had got a month's leave from his duties in that capacity to take a hand in what fighting might occur, was a sort of "odd man" on Sir Sam's staff. He never was oppressed with shyness, and when Sir Sam spoke of his wish to communicate with the left brigade, he put in his word. "I'm an idle man, sir; won't you send me across to General Appleyard to tell him what you want him to do?"

"Very well, Beresford," replied Sir Sam; "I want you to get over as quickly as may be; but you'd better make a bit of a detour to the rear before you cross the valley. By crossing below the bend, you'll avoid most of the fire that is sweeping the direct way across."

"All right, sir," said Bill, with a wink of the eye on the chiefs off side that seemed to say, "I think I see myself detouring."

He took his sword-belt in a couple of holes and started. To begin with, he had to clamber into the valley down the face of an all but perpendicular precipice, on the projections of which the Afghan shells were striking with malign freedom. Looking down from the upper edge I watched him complete the descent, and then start on the dangerous journey across the valley. No doubt he was making good speed; but it looked to me, anxious as I was, as if he were sauntering. Now and then he was hidden altogether by the smoke and dust of an exploding shell.

Cool hand he was, to be sure! When he reached the hither bank of the Khyber stream, he deliberately sat himself down on a stone, and unlaced his boots, took them and his stockings off, and waded the stream barefoot. Having crossed, he sat down and replaced these articles of attire—how abominably particular he seemed, sitting right in the fairway of that belch of fire, about the correct lacing of his ankle boots!

Finally, he lit a cigarette, resumed his tramp across the rest of the valley, and clambering up the rocks bounding its farther side, disappeared among Appleyard's red-coats. That officer was already committed to an attack, so Bill remained with his force and took part in the effort in which Birch and Swettenham went down.

When Sir Sam Browne was halted in Jellalabad, and there was no chance of any further fighting that winter, Bill went back to Simla to his duties about the Viceroy. Presently I, too, tired of the inaction in the Khyber, and travelling down country to Calcutta, and voyaging across the Bay of Bengal to Rangoon, went up the Irrawaddy River into native Burmah, bound for Mandalay, the capital of King Theebaw. While "worshipping the Golden Feet" there, and investigating the eccentricities of the monarch who not long after lost his throne, a telegram came to me from London, ordering me with all speed to South Africa, where the Zulu war had broken out and where the massacre of Isandlwana had just occurred.

Hard on it came a message from Bill, telling he too was off to Zululand, and proposing we should travel down there together.

I wired him back a rendezvous at Aden, the port at the mouth of the Red Sea whence once a month a steamer starts on the voyage along the east coast of Africa as far as Zanzibar; from which place there is connection with Port Durban in Natal by another steamer.

Down the Irrawaddy, across the Bay of Bengal, athwart Hindustan to Kurrachee at the mouth of the Indus I hurried; at Kurrachee caught the steamer for Aden, and at Aden there was Bill, impatiently grilling in that extinct volcano-crater till the Zanzibar packet should start. We dodged into every little obscure Portuguese-negro port along that coast—Quillimane, Mozambique, Magadoxa, Melinda, Lourenço Marquez—stagnant, fever-stricken, half barbarous places where, as it seemed, nobody was either quite black or quite white.

We reached Port Durban about the middle of April 1879, to find its roadstead crowded with the transports that had brought the reinforcements out from England, and its hotels crammed with officers of all ranks and all branches of the services.

General "Fred" Marshall, an old friend of Beresford and myself, commanded the regular cavalry brigade, and Bill hoped for a berth on his staff. But a better billet fell to him. Far up in the Transvaal Sir Evelyn Wood's little brigade had just gained a brilliant victory over some 20,000 Zulus, who had made a desperate attack on its position. Colonel Redvers Buller commanded Wood's irregular volunteer cavalry, and in the recent fight his staff officer, Major Ronald Campbell, had been killed. It was a peculiar and difficult post, and Campbell was a man whom it was not easy to succeed. The assignment rested mainly with Marshall, and on the night of our arrival, he, knowing Beresford better than most men then did, named him for the post.

Full of elation;—Bill because of being chosen for a duty that assured him responsibility and plenty of fighting; I because my chum had so fallen on his feet—we returned to our hotel. As we sat a while in the public room before retiring, there entered a couple of men far from sober. At first, they were civil, and told us that one was the second officer, the other the ship's surgeon, of a transport in the roadstead. Presently the sailor-man's mood changed, and he became grossly insulting to Beresford; who for a while treated him good-humouredly. At last, the fellow said he believed Bill was a coward. Then Bill quietly rose, and simply requested the nautical person to "come outside."

I did not half like the business, for the sailor was a big slab-sided fellow; whereas Bill is one of the light weights, and it was not pleasant to think of his carrying a black eye to his new appointment. But intervention did not seem possible; and it remained for the doctor and myself to "see fair." In front of the hotel was a garden studded with rose-bushes. At it they went hammer and tongs; Bill fending off the big sailor's "ugly rush" with skill and coolness—he had not been at Eton for nothing. In the third round the sailor was down, his head in a rose-bush, and Bill sitting thereon—the head, not the bush.

The sailor did not want any more; everyone shook hands round, and perhaps there was a drink of conciliation. Bill next day went off up country to his billet; and not long after I joined Wood's force up at Kambula. I found Bill too busy to do more than give me a hurried hand-shake. He was Buller's only staff-officer, and the force Buller commanded, about a thousand strong, was the strangest congeries imaginable. It consisted of broken gentlemen, of runagate sailors, of fugitives from justice, of the scum of the South African towns, of stolid Africanders, of Boers whom the Zulus had driven from their farms.

Almost every European nationality was represented; there were a few Americans, some good, some bad; a Greaser; a Chilian; several Australians; and a couple of Canadian voyageurs from somewhere in the Arctic regions. There were Frenchmen who could not speak a word of English, and Channel Islanders whose *patois* neither Englishmen nor Frenchmen could fully understand. One and all were volunteers, recruited for the campaign at the pay of five shillings a day. What added to the complication was that the force comprised a dozen or more sub-commands, each originally, and still to some extent a separate and distinct unit.

There were "Baker's Horse," and "D'Arcy's Horse," and "Beddington's Horse," and "Ferreira's Horse," and so on; each body asserting a certain distinctive independence. Beresford had to arrange all details, keep the duty rosters, inspect the daily parades and the reconnaissance detachments, accompany the latter, lead them if there was any fighting, restrain the rash, hearten the funkers, and be in everything Buller's right-hand man. The volunteer officers, some zealous, some sluggish, some cantankerous, were, as regarded any knowledge of duty, for the most part quite useless. In effect the force, which in numerical strength reckoned as a brigade, was "run" by those two men—Redvers Buller and Bill Beresford.

Buller was a silent, saturnine, bloodthirsty man, as resolute a fighter as ever drew breath—a born leader of men—who ruled his heterogeneous command with a rod of iron. Beresford, to the full as keen a fighter and as firm in compelling obedience, was of a different temperament. He was cheery; with his ready Irish wit he had a vein of genial yet jibing badinage that kept queer-tempered fellows in good humour while it pricked them into obedience. In fine he disclosed the rare gift of managing men—of evoking without either friction or fuss the best that was in them.

And, strangest wonder of all wonders, the fellow whom all men had regarded as the most harum-scarum of mortals—the most "through-other," to use a curious Scotch expression—was found possessed of a real genius for order and system. I admired him excessively in his novel development, but must confess that, being selfish, I did not enjoy it. For he was very busy and I was rather idle, and I grumbled at the deprivation of the brightening of my life that had been contributed by the humour and gaiety of his leisure time.

The campaign, on which almost at its outset had fallen the shadow of the poor Prince Imperial's hapless fate, drawled sluggishly along, till at length as, on the 1st of June, the column wound down into the valley from the bluff of Etonganeni, there lay stretched out beyond the silver sparkle of the river among the trees, the broad plain on whose bosom lay the Royal Kraal of Ulundi, encircled by its satellites. Over the green face of the great flat there flitted what, seen through the heat-haze, seemed dark shadows, but which the field-glass revealed as the *impis* of

Cetewayo practising their manoeuvres.

There are times when the keenest fighting man is not sorry that between his enemy and himself there lies a distance of ten miles. Whether in the spirit or only in the stupid deed, those Zulus were quixotic in the chivalry of their manner of fighting. At Isandlwana only had they been ruses. At Kambula, at Ginghilovo, they had marched straight up into the eye of our fire; at Ulundi they held their hands while we scrambled in dislocation through the broken ground that was the vestibule to the plain; waited with calm patience till our square was methodically formed and locked up; then, after the short hesitation that seemed to ask that question, "Are you quite ready now, gentlemen?" they came at us with surpassing valiantness and a noble ardour, as over the fire-swept plain sped the whirlwind of their converging attack.

There were cynics in our force who smiled grimly and quoted Bosquet's historical sneer, as they watched the evolutions of the *impis* in the hazy distance. Magnificent in their swift precision those evolutions certainly were; but it was not war that the Zulu braves should be wheeling and massing and deploying away there on the plain, instead of taking us at a disadvantage as the long baggage-cumbered column painfully toiled through the dense bush that filled the valley for which we had forsaken the bare upland of the *veldt*.

Cetewayo was hesitating, to meet the proverbial fate of the hesitator. He sent in the sword of the poor Prince Imperial; and later came from him a drove of cattle, the live spoil of Isandlwana. But he would not definitely consent to the terms offered him; yet he refrained from absolutely refusing them. When the *laager* was formed on the pleasant slope stretching up from the rippling Umvaloosi, two days were accorded him in which to make up his mind.

Meantime our attitude was that of vigilant quiescence. The *laager* was roughly entrenched; the guns were got into position; the outposts were strengthened; and arms and ammunition were carefully inspected. During the advance the commands of Newdigate and Wood had marched apart; now for the first time they were united, or at least disjoined only by a subdivision of the *laager*, and there was much visiting to and fro; for it was comparative leisure time for all save Buller's irregulars, who from beginning to end of the campaign may be said to have been on the chronic scout. Some of us went bathing in the Umvaloosi, but had to "lave that"—a pun is not intended—because of a dropping fire from Zulus concealed in the crannies of a rocky hillock or *kopjie*, just across the river from the camp. Not alone for the bathers was this fire a nuisance; a part of the *laager* was within range of the Martini-Henrys got at Isandlwana, which the Zulus on the *kopjie* were using; and one or two casualties occurred.

We had good information as to Cetewayo's strength, thanks to the brave Dutch trader who was his prisoner, and whom he had utilised to write the communications he sent to Lord Chelmsford; at the foot of the last letter the honest fellow, disregarding the risk, had written—"Use caution, he has 20,000 men here." But it was desirable, in view of the contingency of Cetewayo proving stubborn, to gain some detailed knowledge of the ground in our front, over which the final advance would have to be made.

So, on the morning of 3rd July, orders were issued that Buller at mid-day should take out his irregulars across the river, and make a reconnaissance of as much of the plain beyond as the Zulus might see fit to permit. He was not to bring on an engagement, since Cetewayo's "close-time" was not yet up; he was to disregard straggling opposition, but was at once to retire in the face of serious resistance.

These droll irregulars never took much pains about parading. Neither smartness nor uniformity was a desideratum. The fellows dressed how they liked, or rather, perhaps, how they could: their only weapon, besides the revolver, a Martini-Henry rifle, each man carried as seemed unto him best, providing that he carried it somehow, somewhere about himself or his pony. The only uniform accoutrement was the *bandoleer* in which the cartridges were carried.

When they got ready, they mounted; when he found around him a reasonable number of mounted men, the leader of the corps started; his fellows followed in files, and the men who were late overtook the detachment at a canter. No man skulked; the majority were keen enough for fighting, and the funkers, if there were any, had to pretend to be as zealous as their comrades.

Buller and Beresford were always in the saddle early, waiting for the firstlings of the muster. Buller's favourite mount was a fiddle-headed, brindled, flat-sided, ewe-necked cob named Punch. He was perhaps the very ugliest horse of his day and generation in all South Africa, but he was also among the most valuable. Although not very fast, his endurance was wonderful; he made nothing of a hundred miles at a stretch, with an occasional "off-saddle" and a roll as the only relief; but it was neither his endurance nor his ugliness that constituted his special value. He was "salted" to the third degree of saltness; he was a veritable "mark mason" among "salted" horses.

Now salt-horse in the South African sense has no affinity with the salt-horse at which sailors grumble. The "salted horse" of the *veldt* is an animal which is proof against the pestilence known as "horse-sickness." He rarely survives the attack; after one attack he is still liable to another, but less liable; he may have three attacks, and if he yet lives, he is of the loftiest aristocracy of "saltness," and proof for all time against horse-sickness. If that were the only ill that horse-flesh is heir to, he would be immortal.

Beresford had lost one horse by a Zulu bullet, another by horse-sickness; but cavalryman and steeplechase rider as he was, he was not the man to be badly mounted. He rode a smart chestnut, with the Irish Birdcatcher white ticks on his withers and flanks. The leader of the irregulars and his staff-officer sat on their horses in front of Evelyn Wood's tent, waiting for their fellows to come on the ground. Wood, standing in his tent-door, chatted to the laconic Buller, while Beresford and "the boy"—young Lysons, Wood's *A.D.C.*, was "the boy"—gossiped a little apart.

Presently Baker came along at the head of his assortment of miscreants; Ferreira leading his particular bandits, was visible in the offing, and Buller, alongside of Baker, headed the procession of horsemen down toward the river, Beresford temporarily remaining to see the turnout complete and close up the command. Before Buller was at the waterside, he had galloped up to the head of the column, for it was his place, as ever, to lead the advance; Buller bringing on the main body behind the scouts.

The arrangements were simple; and there was no delay down by the Umvaloosi bank, where the accelerated fire from the Zulus in the *kopjie* over against them whistled over the heads of the horsemen; over whom too screamed the shells from the guns in front of the *laager* that were being thrown in among the crags where the Zulus lurked.

The spray of the Umvaloosi dashed from the horse-hoofs of the irregulars, as they forded the river on the right of the *kopjie*, and then bending to the left round it, took it in reverse. The Zulus who had been holding it had not cared much for the shell fire, ensconced among the rocks as they were, but were quick to notice the risk they ran of being cut off by the movement of the horsemen, and made a bolt of it Beresford's fellows galloped hard to intercept them, Bill well in front, sending his chestnut along as if he were "finishing" in front of the stand at Sandown.

The Zulu *induna*, bringing up the rear of his fleeing detachment, turned on the lone man who had so outridden his followers. A big man, even for a Zulu, the ring round his head proved him a veteran. The muscles rippled on his glistening black shoulders as he compacted himself behind his huge flecked shield of cowhide, marking his distance for the thrust of the gleaming *assegai* held at arm's length over the great swart head of him. Bill steadied his horse a trifle, just as he was wont to do before the take off for a big fence; within striking distance he made him swerve a bit to the left—he had been heading straight for the Zulu, as if he meant to ride him down.

The spear flashed out like the head of a cobra as it strikes; the sabre carried at "point one" clashed with it, and seemed to curl round it; the spear-head was struck aside; the horseman delivered "point two" with all the vigour of his arm, his strong seat, and the impetus of his galloping horse; and lo! in the twinkling of an eye, the sabre's point was through the shield, and half its length buried in the Zulu's broad chest. The brave *induna* was a dead man before he dropped; the sword drawing out of his heart as he fell backward. His *assegai* stands now in the corner of Bill's mother's drawing-room.

Beresford's Zulu was the only man slain with the "white arm" in hand-to-hand combat during the day, but of the fugitives whom the dead *induna* had commanded, several fell under the fire of the fellows who followed that chief's slayer. The surviving Zulus ran into the nearest military *kraal*, Delyango. Out of it the irregulars rattled them, as well as the few Zulus who had been garrisoning it. A detachment had been left behind—a fortunate precaution taken by Buller—to cover the retreat by holding the *kopjie* in the rear; and then the force—Beresford and his scouts still leading, the main body spread out on rather a broad front— galloped on through the long grass across the open, bending rather leftward in the direction of the Nodwengo, the next military *kraal* in the direction of Ulundi.

In front of the horsemen there kept retiring at a pace regulated by theirs, about two hundred Zulus, all who were then visible anywhere on the face of the plain. These shunned Nodwengo, leaving it on their right, and heading straight for Ulundi. The irregulars drew rein long enough for a patrol to ride into Nodwengo and report it empty. Then the horses having got their wind, the rapid advance recommenced. It really seemed a straight run in for Buller and Beresford as they set their horses' heads for Ulundi and galloped on. The idea had occurred to many in the force that Cetewayo must have abandoned his capital and withdrawn his army into the hill country close behind Ulundi.

Those irregular horsemen had no very keen sense of discipline, and in a gallop, a forward gallop especially, were rather prone to get out of hand. Buller's hardest task was to restrain this impulse, and it was well that day that he was exerting himself all he knew to curb the ardour of his fellows. Beresford's advance-detachment, scouts as they were, were of course straggled out rather casually over the whole front.

Everything seemed prosperous. No enemy showed anywhere save the two hundred fugitive Zulus, falling back ahead of our fellows at the long easy run which takes the Zulu over the ground with surprising speed and which he can keep up hour

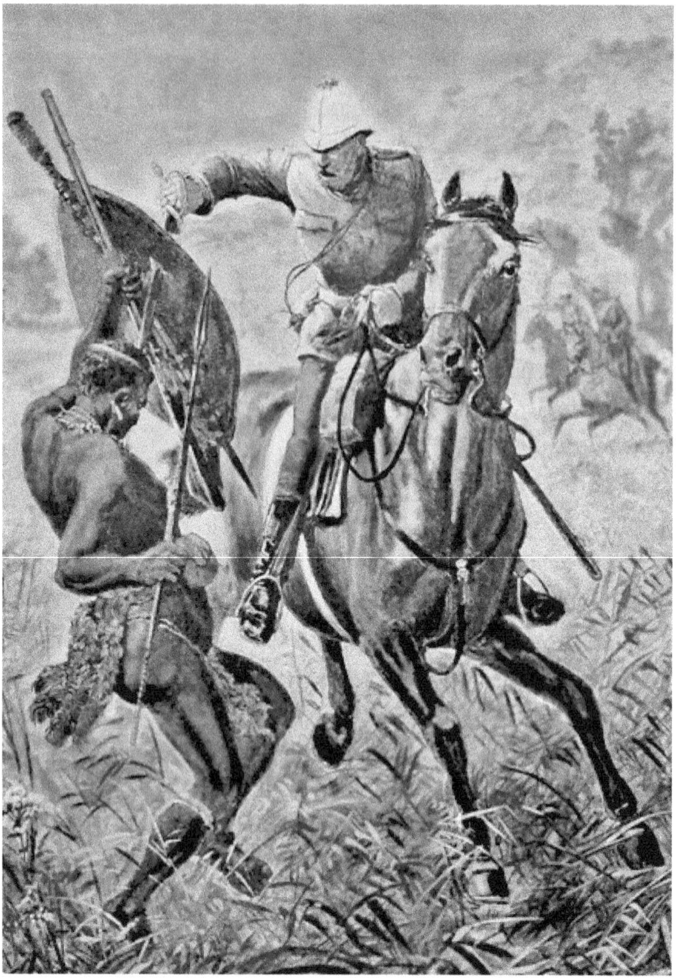

after hour without a symptom of distress.

Their flight was a calculated snare; those fugitives were simply a wily decoy. Suddenly from out a deep, sharply-cut watercourse crossing the plain, and invisible at two hundred yards' distance, sprang up a long line of Zulus, some two thousand strong, confronting at once and flanking the horsemen. Simultaneously the whole plain around them flashed up into vivid life. Hordes of Zulus had been lying hidden in the long grass. Buller's alert eye had caught the impending danger, and his voice had rung out the command "Retire" ere yet the bullets of the sudden Zulu volley whistled through and over his command.

Three men went down smitten by the fire. Two were killed on the spot and never stirred; we found their bodies next day shockingly mangled. The third man's horse slipped up in the abrupt turn, and his rider for the moment lay stunned. But Beresford, riding away behind his retreating party, looked back at this latter man, and saw him move up into a sitting posture.

He who would succour in such a crisis must not only be a brave man, but also a prompt man, quick to decide and as quick to act The issue of life or death hangs at such a time on the gain or waste of a moment. The Zulus, darting out from the watercourse, were perilously close to the poor fellow; but Beresford, used on the racecourse to measuring distance with the eye, thought he might just do it, if he were smart and lucky. Galloping back to the wounded man, he dismounted, and ordered him to get on his pony.

The wounded man, dazed as he was, even in his extremity was not less full of self-abnegation than was the man who was risking his own life in the effort to save his. He bade Beresford remount and go; why, he said in his simple manly logic—why should two die when death was inevitable but to one? Then it was that the quaint resourceful humour of his race supplied Beresford with the weapon that prevailed over the wounded man's unselfishness. The recording angel perhaps did not record the oath that buttressed his threatening mien when he swore with clenched fist that he would punch the wounded man's head if he did not allow his life to be saved.

This droll argument prevailed. Bill partly lifted, partly hustled the man into his saddle, then scrambled up somehow in front of him, and set the good little beast agoing after the other horsemen. He only just did it; another moment's delay and both must have been *assegaied*. As it was, the swift-footed Zulus chased them up the slope, and the least mistake made by the pony must have been fatal. Indeed, as Beresford was the first gratefully to admit, there was a critical moment when their escape would have been impossible, but for the cool courage of Sergeant O'Toole, who rode back to the rescue, shot down Zulu after Zulu with his revolver as they tried to close in on the rather helpless pair, and then aided Beresford in keeping the wounded man in the saddle until the safety of the *laager* was attained.

There was danger right up till then; for the hordes of Zulus obstinately hung on the flanks and rear of Buller's command, and the irregulars had over and over again to shoot men down at close quarters with the revolver; more than once the fighting was hand-to-hand and they had to club their rifles. If the Zulus had kept to their own weapon, the *assegai*, the loss among Buller's men would have been very severe; but they had extensively armed themselves with rifles that had fallen into their hands at Isandlwana, with the proper handling of which they were unfamiliar. They pursued right up to their own bank of the Umvaloosi, and blazed away at our fellows long after the river was between them and us.

Of course, cumbered with a wounded and fainting man occupying his saddle while he perched on the pommel, Beresford was unable to do anything toward self-protection, and over and over again on the return ride, he and the man behind him were in desperate strait, and but for O'Toole and other comrades must have gone down. When they alighted in the *laager* you could not have told whether it was rescuer or rescued who was the wounded man, so smeared was Beresford with borrowed blood. It was one of Ireland's good days; if at home she is the "distressful country," wherever bold deeds are to be done and military honour to be gained, no nation carries the head higher out of the dust.

If originally Norman, the Waterford family have been Irish now for six centuries, and Bill Beresford is an Irishman in heart and blood. Sergeant Fitzmaurice, the wounded man who displayed a self-abnegation so fine, was an Irishman also; and Sergeant O'Toole—well, I think one runs no risk in the assumption that an individual who bears that name, in spite of all temptation, remains an Irishman. So, in this brilliant little episode the Green Isle had it all to herself.

It will ever be one of the pleasantest memories of my life, that the good fortune was mine to call the attention of Sir Evelyn Wood to Bill Beresford's conduct on this occasion. By next mail his recommendation for the Victoria Cross went home to England; and when he and I reached Plymouth Sound at the close of our voyage, the Prince of Wales, who was then in the Sound with Lord Charles Beresford, was the first to send aboard the *Dublin Castle* the news that Her Majesty had been pleased to honour the recommendation. Lord William was commanded to Windsor to receive the reward "for Valour" from the hands of his sovereign.

But there is something more to be told. Honest as valiant, he had already declared that he could not in honour receive any recognition of the service it had been his good fortune to perform, unless that recognition were shared in by Sergeant O'Toole, who he persisted in maintaining deserved infinitely greater credit than any that might attach to him. Queen Victoria can appreciate not less than soldierly valour, soldierly honesty, generosity, and modesty; and so it came about that the next *Gazette* after Lord William Beresford's visit to Windsor contained the announcement that the proudest reward a soldier of our Empire can aspire to had been conferred on Sergeant Edmund O'Toole, of Baker's Horse.

CHARLES EDWIN FRIPP

Reminiscences of the Zulu War, 1879
By Charles E. Fripp.

The news of the fatal fight of January 22nd, 1879, where, under the shadow of the lion-shaped hill of Isandhlwana, twenty thousand fearless Zulus swept over the British camp and annihilated its brave defenders, reached England on February 10th, awakening the people and government to the magnitude of the task of subduing Cetywayo and his people.

A week later transports were busy taking on board troops of all arms and munitions of war for South Africa, whither I proceeded with the first reinforcements as special artist to the *Graphic*, leaving London on February 19th, and landing at Durban, Natal, on March 20th.

It is needless, and not within the scope of this article, to narrate in detail how the first invasion of Zululand came to a standstill owing to the repulse of the centre column and the inadequacy of the force employed: the brilliant defence of Rorke's Drift was the solitary bright point in the campaign.

Colonel Wood's left column remained halted at Kambula,

keeping his communications open; but Colonel Pearson, with the right column, after gaining a small advantage over the Zulus on the Insandusani, was cut off from his base on the Tugela and practically beleaguered at Etshowe; panic spread in Natal; the border and other towns were put into a state of defence by their inhabitants to withstand the expected invasion by the Zulus; but Cetywayo, influenced by the good Bishop Colenso, refrained from this counterblow.

The relief of Etshowe being the necessary preliminary to the second invasion of Zululand premeditated, the first reinforcements landed were at once marched to the Tugela to form a column for this purpose; and at this point commences this article, compiled from notes made on the spot at the time.

The column for the relief of Tyoe, better known as "Etshowe," had assembled under General Lord Chelmsford on the Zulu side of the Tugela River at Fort Tenedos, not many miles from the sea. The stream of water is broad and deep, but like most African rivers there is a dangerous bar obstructing the entrance. On the evening of March 28th, the rain was falling in torrents as I stood with my horse on the Natal bank among the heaps of boxes and

In Laager.

sacks, and surrounded by officers, horses, and detached parties of soldiers awaiting transportation across the turbid stream by the pontoon ferry; Kaffirs, nude and perspiring, lustily handled the heaps of provisions and stores, and officers and men of the indefatigable Naval Brigade worked from earliest dawn to late at night ferrying the ever re-accumulating crowd of men, animals, and stores across the river.

For some miles the land was undulating, covered with long grass, with bush growing only in the gullies; but this growth was denser ahead and to the right nearer the sea, which gleamed brightly in intervals of sunlight that broke through the clouds. The order of march was firstly an "advanced division," then came a column of one hundred and fifteen bullock waggons, flanked by "Natal Native Contingent" battalions and other irregulars, and lastly a "rear division." Each "division" consisted of about two battalions of infantry and a detachment of the Naval Brigade, which provided the only artillery accompanying the force—*viz.*, two seven-pounders, two Gatlings, and some rocket tubes.

This day we marched about ten miles, and went into *laager* in the afternoon, near the Inyoni River, throwing up a shelter trench outside the enclosure, which was much crowded. At night it rained again, but I slept like a top under the waggon in my waterproof, in spite of the water which ran over the surface of the slope.

The greater part of the 31st was employed in crossing the Amatikulu River, the waters of which were too high to attempt fording last night. It is a fine stream with sandy bottom, high banks with tall reeds on the water's edge. The whole force only advanced two miles, and the troops were formed in readiness to resist an attack during the operation of crossing the drift (which took eight hours), for the enemy actually crossed the river on our left, but subsequently retired without attempting anything further. It was generally reported that the Zulus were on three sides of us, the rear alone being open, but since leaving Fort Tenedos only one party had been sighted up to this day.

LEAVING THE OLD CAMP AT GINGHILOVO

THE NAVAL BRIGADE IN ACTION

The morning of April 2nd was grey, when at reveille I turned out of my sleeping quarters close to a corner of the *laager* occupied by part of the Naval Brigade; the sailors were lighting their fires outside the trenches, preparing the morning meal, all hands helping in their habitual cheery way; smoke rose slowly in the air all round the *laager*, water fatigue and other parties moved up and down the slope, cheerful shouts and the chattering of the natives came from all sides.

The bullocks were being led out to feed, when the hum of an alarm spread itself over the camp, a strange, low, all-pervading murmur, a sound of rushing, of trampling, hurried footsteps, a sound of moving bodies, but not of voices, excepting some isolated sharp word of command.

I do not recollect hearing the long-drawn note of the bugle denoting the alarm, customary in the British Army; but suddenly the voices were hushed, succeeded by a hurried trample that seemed to throb in the air. From all sides men streamed into camp; the trenches became full of figures bobbing up and down as the accoutrements were picked up; and there was much hasty buttoning and buckling on. An occasional shot fell on the ear; a bushy-bearded sailor close to me carefully picked up his cooking-pot and carried it to the entrenchment already lined by his comrades.

After an hour's engagement, commencing at 6 a.m., the enemy had received a severe repulse, with trifling loss to our force; but I was surprised to see how few dead lay where I had observed the fighting—though, being scattered over a large area of long grass, the number was difficult to estimate: the nearest body I saw was fifty yards from the trenches, and nowhere did I see them piled together.

The head of the relieving column did not reach the fort at Etshowe until after sunset on April 3rd, and it was growing dusk when the men of the 60th were greeted by the cheers of the garrison. I remember the figures of the relieved soldiers standing on the parapet in dark outline against the rich golden sky. The rearguard did not get in till 11 p.m., and it must have been midnight before all was still. The night was beautiful, and for hours after dark lines of troops were moving into camp, their accoutrements glinting in the light of the camp fires, as, tired and silent, they marched to the position assigned, dug their trenches, and after soldiers' fare, lay down to rest in their great-coats.

All the mounted men under Lord Chelmsford moved out of camp next morning to attack Dabulamanzi in his large *kraal*, seven miles distant from Etshowe. There were mounted infantry in their red coats and tanned helmets, volunteers clad in serviceable cord clothing and slouch felt hats, native irregulars similarly clad, but besides rifle and *banderole*, having their *assegais* in a sheath bound to the saddle, and wearing no boots rode with the big toe only in the stirrup; all were mounted on small but strong African horses. The country through which we passed was down-like, covered with long African grass, dense bush growing in large patches in the valleys and hollows.

Scouts and detached parties, one of which I accompanied, spread out over the open, and we soon lost sight of the main bodies. The landscape was closely scanned for signs of the enemy in vain, and I thought I would do a little scouting on my own account and make for some other parties to the right. I soon, however, found myself alone, but luckily met two volunteers who had lost their reckoning, and together we made a smart canter in the direction where I had last seen one of our detachments—for it was not particularly safe to be roaming about out of touch. Every bit of bush or gully we came to was eyed suspiciously and investigated before crossing; but there were no signs of the enemy, which I think was satisfactory to all three of us.

After some hard riding we sighted two more irregular horsemen leading a Zulu prisoner with a rein round his neck between them; and following, we shortly afterwards joined a small party of horsemen, one of whom was a thickset man clad in the ordinary cord clothing of Englishmen in South Africa. He wore a short beard, and clear grey eyes looked out from under the broad brim of his felt hat: this person was John Dunn, known as Cetywayo's "white man," and he sat in his saddle, rifle butt on

Destruction of Dabulamanzi's kraal, April 4
Fripp centre left sketching

thigh, quietly speaking to the prisoner, a young fellow of fine physique and steady fearless bearing.

John Dunn was married to a Zulu wife, and was head of a small tribe; and if, as I understand was the case, Cetywayo on the outbreak of the war allowed him with his people and cattle to leave the country, Dunn could have played a more honourable part than to have joined Lord Chelmsford's column, assisting by his local knowledge and his fighting tribesmen.

It is related that the king asked him if he would fight the English in case of war; and on his reply in the negative, he was told that had his answer been otherwise he would not have been believed, and most likely would have been "eaten up." It is further said that Dunn was present when war was being debated at the king's *kraal*, and he was asked whether the English could fight the Zulus: he asked for a large vessel of water to be brought to him, then, dipping his finger into it, he let a drop fall on the ground and replied, "The drop on the ground is the Zulu nation, the vessel of water is the English."

When we met Dunn, we were close upon Dabulamanzi's *kraal*, situated among huge rounded slopes; in the rear were drawn up irregulars, mounted infantry, and natives dismounted were busy setting fire to the huts and stockade. Colonel Crealock with his glasses was observing a hill, where from, time to time we could see little puffs of smoke, followed by distant reports and the whistle of bullets overhead. Being at a long range (over one thousand yards), this fire was unanswered except by Dunn, who lay on his back and fired a few shots in return. Dabulamanzi was a first-class rifle-shot, and it was suggested that he and Dunn were having a match.

According to the prisoner, Dabulamanzi had his cattle the other side of the hill, and it seems to have been his intention to have us follow him into an awkward corner; but our force being small, the only mounted men of the column being our leaders, and satisfied that the *kraal* was destroyed, we turned our backs upon the column of dark smoke and rode leisurely back to Etshowe, the natives bearing various articles suspended from their saddles, plunder from this and other *kraals*, the smoke from which rose on many hillsides.

Scouts and detached parties

Colonel Pearson's column evacuated Etshowe this morning, but his march seems to have been leisurely; his cattle, reported poor, may account for the delay partially, as his rearguard only left as we returned.

Lord Chelmsford, having successfully relieved Colonel Pearson's force in Etshowe, after inflicting a severe defeat upon the enemy, whose loss must have been close upon a thousand killed, and finally having thoroughly cleared that part of the country, returned with his staff to the Tugela on April 7th, and of course was followed by the batch of special correspondents, of which I formed a humble unit.

★★★★★★★★★★★★★★★★

In those days the railroad only went to Botha's Hill, half-way between Durban and Pietermaritzburg, where was also an accumulation of stores awaiting further transport. On a grassy slope were rows of the white tents and picketed horses of the King's

ESHOWE FORT

Dragoon Guards, who were travelling by easy stages to allow the horses to get their land-legs after the long sea voyage, riding on next day.

I and a travelling companion arrived the same evening at Pietermaritzburg, passing through a somewhat bare-looking grassy country, most productive of ant-hills, without adventure, excepting that I trod inadvertently upon a dangerous snake, a black mamba, and performed an involuntary war-dance on the reptile, to the detriment of its health. After a week's delay in this most charming little town, we resumed our slow journey up country, sometimes riding, sometimes driving; but we always found Natal a pleasant country to travel in, spite of the bad inns, or "hotels," as the very meanest of them are termed.

On May 5th we reached a little place called Ladysmith, where we had to go under canvas, and draw rations, as we were entitled to do by the courtesy of the military authorities; and having reduced my kit to its smallest dimensions, consisting only of blankets, a few cooking-pots, and a change of clothes, I started off again with my Kaffir servant Jim, and (sleeping in the open) reached Dundee on the 12th,

We were now on the extreme western border of Zululand, and here the troops of General Newdigate's division had been collected, with transport and stores in different camps, including Dundee, Landmann's Drift, Doornberg and Conference Hill. Each of these places I visited in turn, and found them all similarly situated and strongly intrenched on the open grassy *veldt*.

On May 31st the first brigade crossed the Blood River—a slow undertaking; the second following on June 1st, on which day the whole column advanced, and *laagering* near the Itelezi mountain, the invasion may be said to have commenced. For days the scouts of the enemy had been seen, some within seven miles of the Blood River; our movements being evidently seen by them. During the afternoon a rumour spread that the Prince Imperial of France, accompanying the British forces as a volunteer, had been killed; it was, however, not credited, for "shaves" were always flying about camp; but when orders in the evening detailed detachments to seek for the corpse of the unfortunate prince, there could be no room for doubt, and the unexpected confirmation of the report was received with lively expressions of regret in the little circle of officers with whom I messed.

General Marshall, accompanied by Major Molyneux, *A.D.C.* to Lord Chelmsford, and Surgeon-Major Scott, with detachments of lancers and natives, left camp on the morning of June 2nd for the Itytyosi River, where the catastrophe had occurred. The country being open undulating *veldt*, it did not take long for the leading horsemen to reach the spot, and a group of two or three in a *donga* (the bed of a watercourse) attracting our attention, we soon gathered round them.

There at our feet lay, deprived of all clothing, the corpse of the son of an emperor who once held the most prominent position in Europe, and of an empress the star of the most brilliant court of that time.

There he lay, the hope of the Napoleons, with the pitiless stabs of the Zulu *assegais* on his fair body uncovered to the hot African sun, save by the waving blades of grass; although one eye was wounded by an *assegai*, the aspect of face and body was peaceful, and, in spite of the customary shallow incision in the abdomen which the Zulu warriors make on the slain, either from superstition or sanitary motives, the corpse was not mutilated. Round his neck, on a fine chain, was a small ornament, the gift of his Imperial mother, the savages having otherwise deprived him of everything. It was in truth a melancholy spectacle to contemplate.

On arriving at camp, the little procession moved through a crowd of soldiers gathered to receive it, and in the evening the troops paraded to attend the burial service—an impressive sight—the lines of soldiers forming in the dusk a dark mass against the gold and purple sky, and in the centre of the troops gleamed dimly the white robes of the officiating chaplain, standing before the gun-carriage whereon lay the corpse of the ill-fated prince.

Colonel Wood's column, which had been moving on our left, was now a couple of miles ahead of us. A soldier of that column was killed when fetching water—a rare instance of that species of warfare in Zululand.

The advance was resumed for a couple of days, *laager* being made hastily each evening, owing to reports of the enemy being concentrated in the vicinity. On the 7th the division encamped on a fine, open piece of country overlooking the Upoko River, and facing a table mountain called "Zungeni," the parched yellow slopes of which were well dotted with dark bush, where we seemed to discern movement, and were speculating on the probable presence of the enemy as three nine-pounders rattled up and unlimbered smartly; the first piece was adjusted, a flash proceeded, the white cloud enveloping gun and detachment as the heavy report struck our ears; with a rushing sound the projectile passed over the valley.

We suddenly saw a little ball of smoke in the distance, and

after a time a dull report reached us; the vicinity where the shell was seen to burst became alive with minute dark specks—"Four thousand yards," said the artillery officer, as he watched through his glass. Another and another shell followed, until five rounds per gun were fired, and the moving specks had all disappeared.

We then learnt that the bush was full of *kraals*, and next day a large force was sent to clear it out. At an early hour the native auxiliaries and mounted men, supported by two battalions of infantry and some guns, left camp, and were soon swarming over the country. I accompanied some volunteers who scouted on the left of the advance through some broken stony country dotted with bush and wild aloes. When some miles out the leading scouts were seen to halt, dismount and fire, puffs of smoke showing the presence of the enemy in some bush-clad precipitous rocks. The boom of a seven-pounder, followed by the rush of a projectile, announced the arrival of supporting artillery on our right.

"*The motionless, listening figure of a sentry.*"

The shells burst over the enemy's cover at fifteen hundred yards range, and speedily silenced their fire, excepting that of one determined individual, who replied to each shell with a musketoon that boomed forth a loud defiance to the guns, un-

HEADQUARTERS, SIX MILES FROM ULUNDI, JULY 3:
"SHALL WE HAVE A FIGHT TOMORROW?"

til a particularly accurate shell seemed to strike the very spot where he was concealed: his loudvoiced weapon was no longer heard in the land, and the advance swept on until we sighted the hills behind Zungeni mountain. Columns of black smoke rose from burning *kraals*; long black lines preceded by swarms of dots slowly wound their way across the sunlit landscape, and showed us that the country was being thoroughly scoured of the enemy. Occasional distant shots fell on the ear, but there were no signs of serious opposition. Our native allies revelled in the glory of burning and destroying without any risk to their black skins, and returned to camp chattering and singing, laden with mealies, strips of meat, and Zulu utensils.

The advance was resumed on June 18th, and the Upoko crossed on the 19th. On Sunday, June 22nd, a halt was made to give rest to the hard-worked troops and cattle; for we had ascended tremendous steeps, and had attained an elevation far above the surrounding country, of which we had frequent grand views, especially in the direction of a fine mountain named Ibabanango.

On the 23rd the circular form of Ulundi, Cetywayo's *kraal*, was just visible to the naked eye over the intervening long undulating ridges; and on the 27th we encamped on the last of the spurs of the great plateaux. Below and between us and the curved shining stream of the Umvolosi River lay a beautiful valley densely clad with bush, mingled with euphorbias and wild aloes; across the river we saw some miles of a large basin open and undulating, the hills enclosing it being partially bush-clad, with larger open *steeps* and mountains behind; and in the open basin we could see the circular forms of large *kraals*, of which one was Ulundi.

★★★★★★★★★★★★★★★★

It was on the eve of the decisive blow of the campaign. From early morn active preparations for the final advance upon Ulundi had been in progress. The great waggons forming the "*laager*" had been drawn up close to one another, leaving no unnecessary gaps, and the strength of the line of defence thus afforded was increased by spade work.

How long the camp may have been wrapt in slumber, or why the senses should have become awakened, it would be difficult to say. I can only recollect that suddenly my senses became keenly alert, and I was wide awake, listening. 'The moon was shining gloriously over the recumbent figures still motionless in sleep around me, and tipping the tented waggons with touches of light.

Instinctively straining my ears, I strove to distinguish a sound above and through the undefined champing noise of cattle, and raising myself on my elbows sought to determine whether a faint murmur as of distant voices was imagination or reality. For a while doubt would predominate, and then, as on a silent breath of night, a multitude of voices seemed to be borne from infinite space, to pass away into nothingness. I rose to my feet.

From overhead the golden moon of Africa flooded the landscape with vague light, and one could dimly distinguish the distant mountains beyond Ulundi. The *krantz* on the farther side of the Mvolosi, overlooking the ford, stood out darkly, with the stream rippling in bright sheen at its base; the extensive bush spread out around us dark and mysterious, and in the open ring of clearing the limbs and remnants of the felled vegetation assumed fantastic, indistinguishable forms under the magic light of the moon. The motionless, listening figure of a sentry stood on a waggon close at hand.

Again, that vague murmur was borne on the night wind in low, harmonious chords, swelling and dying to rise again clearer than before: with ever-increasing distinctness thousands of exultant voices rose and fell in perfect rhythm faintly but defiantly upon our ears.

It was the war chant of thousands of Zulu warriors, whose sonorous voices were pouring forth songs of devotion to their king through the stillness of night, swaying their supple bodies and gleaming weapons in fierce unison with the beating feet under the same calm moon shining on our silent camp. Louder and louder grew the song, and although miles distant one could

A ZULU REGIMENT ATTACKING

hear the higher voices prevail above the resonant roar of the bass; indeed, it seemed as if the singers were nearing the camp, and some of the men stood quietly to their arms; but after some waiting there seemed no probability of an attack, and though the weird chorus and the beauty of the night exercised an unexampled fascination, we lay down, and lulled by the low confused murmur of the cattle in the *laager*, again fell asleep.

The morning following, the sun was shining faintly through the morning mist when I arose. The camp, roused without bugle-call, had been astir at an early hour, and the troops forming the fighting square were already preparing to fall in; but knowing that the crossing of the drift would occupy a considerable time, I was able to attend leisurely to the feeding of my pony and self, whilst the column quietly formed up and moved off through the bush towards the Mvolosi.

It must have been past eight o'clock when I splashed through the river, speedily overtaking some Scotch carts whose escorts were strenuously endeavouring to urge forward the decrepit bullocks, a transport officer anxiously watching and directing their efforts.

"Endeavouring to urge forward the decrepit bullocks."

Passing by the *krantz*, the huge square of red coats was visible to me about a mile off, moving slowly over the undulating plain of yellow sunburnt grass, the arms and accoutrements glinting brightly in the sun.

On our left great parklike slopes irregularly dotted with bush showed as yet no signs of the enemy's presence: on our right, a column of black smoke rapidly increasing in volume and intensity rose from a huge circular *kraal*, Unodwengo, which had been fired by our cavalry that was moving over the rolling plain beyond. The square was easily overtaken, as it was frequently compelled to halt so that the carts, which dribbled out of the rear like a tail as the cattle became fatigued, might resume their places in the formation.

Having joined a small knot of officers who were scanning the hills on our left front with field-glasses, I was enabled, being possessed of a keen sight, to call the attention of one to some dark specks on the aloe-dotted summit of a large slope. "Aloes," said he at first; but a general concentration of the glasses in that direction proved that the "aloes" were moving down the slope and were followed shortly by the appearance of a thin undulating line on the ridge, succeeded by others to right and left, all conforming to a general movement down the slopes towards us; and other similar lines appeared by degrees from over the other ridges on the hills to our left.

The square was now halted, and some men began to pull down the wattled fences of a small *kraal* close at hand; but in a very short while the advance was resumed, and the force took up a position on the top of a swelling rise, marked by the brown walls of a dismantled house, said to be an old mission station, whence we could see Ulundi and the other great *kraals* of Likazi and Umpanbongwena.

Firing, far away on our right, now fell on our ears; and our mounted irregulars, like dots in the distance, could be seen retiring, and returning the fire of a swarm of similar black dots rapidly following across the grassy slopes, now overshadowed by a huge column of dark smoke rising from the burning Unodwengo. Some men were busy with picks pulling down the mud walls of the old house, the guns took position outside the angles of the square, and I found a good berth on the top of an ammunition cart to get a good all-round view.

Preceded by an irregular line of skirmishers who opened a desultory fire at great distance, the enemy on our left had moved down the hills in a loose line of companies, followed by others in file in rear: on our front the Zulus were streaming out of distant Ulundi like a black thread, the head of the column disappearing for a time in a dip of the ground to reappear as a swarm of specks on a nearer rise. Our artillery now opened fire, and the gun nearest to me dropped a shrapnel right on the swarm heading out of Ulundi, the extreme clearness of the atmosphere permitting one to see the bullets strike up the dust, and the little black figures bend forward as they swept on towards us, though I imagined some dropped.

Now and again a bullet sighed overhead as I watched the beautiful advance of the enemy rapidly spreading over the undulations, disappearing and reappearing as the inequalities were traversed; and wherever the white smoke of the artillery did not interfere with the view, there could one see the attackers steadily approaching, heedless of bursting projectiles, and gradually assuming an open order increasing in depth as the line of battle surrounding the square became more and more contracted. In the pauses between the artillery discharges, a faint distant murmur could be heard, but otherwise the attacking line pushed forward in silence.

Our mounted men, regulars and irregulars, retiring before the enemy, filed into the square where the infantry stood motionless in the sunlight regarding the magnificent order of the attack. The firing of the Zulus soon began to increase on the sides of the square farther from me, the bullets coming pretty freely, humming, whistling and whirring according to the nature of the projectiles of their many-patterned armament; yet, although the interior of the square was crammed with ammunition and water-carts, ambulances, bullocks, drivers, native auxiliaries, and the dismounted cavalry with their horses, and presented an enormous target, the effect appeared to be nil. Then the crisp crackle of our own rifle fire began to reply, and the white smoke began to pile up overhead, excepting on that part of the square where my position enabled me to obtain the best view.

On this face stood some companies of the 94th, with the colour party of that regiment, the line prolonged to the right by a regiment of General Wood's Division—the 57th, I believe. Some men were calmly digging a shelter trench in rear of the line; those in the ranks intently watching the approach of the enemy, whose dark figures became more and more distinct at each ridge as they reappeared out of the intervening hollow. The distance to the top of the nearest slope in our front was here about three hundred yards, and the moment was eagerly awaited when the attackers should crown this rise, the kneeling front rank craning forward, the rear rank settling their feet in the proper position to get a firm footing when the order to commence fire should be given.

There was not long to wait: dark heads began to show themselves above the long line of the opposite ridge, and step by step, as the leading line breasted the last bit of rise, the nude bodies rose to our view, some upright, some crouching; then a new line of dark heads followed them, and more steadily followed those, and it looked as if the whole slope would be inundated with black figures descending towards us; but at a well-chosen moment our soldiers' rifles were levelled, and volleys of bullets swept across the hollow to tear up the dust among the enemy in a most uncomfortable manner. Volley succeeded volley, and through the gaps in the drifting haze of smoke arising from the firing line, I could see the dark figures sink into the long grass.

Frequent puffs of white smoke on the ridge told of a return fire; but the marksmanship was miserable, and the bullets sang overhead, probably doing most execution amongst the shooters' friends on the other sides of the square, though some came sufficiently close to induce me to regard the exhortation of a gunner to descend from my post of observation. The infantry, in whose

Returning into the square.

immediate rear I now stood, fixed bayonets, and the digging party joined the ranks; pauses were now allowed between each volley, and as the smoke cleared away, deliberate independent firing commenced under good control.

Then the Zulus, the mass of whom lay still under shelter of the slope, suddenly rose and moved forward, invited thereto by the slackening of the fire; but an increased pelting of bullets showered on them checked the movement, though it did not prevent daring individuals from dashing down the slope and throwing themselves down into the long grass, concealed by which they would creep forward and maintain a fire that would have proved very deadly had they not been such very bad marksmen. As it was, they only attracted the eager attention of some young soldier, who would appeal to his officer—"There's one, sir! mayn't I have a shot, sir?" a request usually granted, much to Tommy's gratification.

"I could see dark figures sink into the long grass."

Again and again, when fire slackened, did the enemy attempt to come over the ridge in force; but each time it proved fruitless, being met with a destructive fire which, it soon became evident, held our adversaries in check; for our fire only continued slowly to keep down the comparatively innocuous fire from the ridge. But on the next face to our left, where more companies of the 94th stood with some of the 21st, a tremendously rapid rifle fire broke out, and a cloud of white vapour rose above the square.

Mounting my pony to look over the firing ranks, I rode in that direction along the rear of the fighting line, but it was impossible to see clearly through the veil of smoke piling up around; yet I could see Lord Chelmsford quietly sitting on his horse as he watched the men rapidly handle their Martini-Henrys and discharge a terrific storm of bullets.

This was without doubt the climax of the engagement; but the density of the smoke making it impossible to distinguish anything transpiring outside the square, I moved to windward again and got a glimpse through the haze of dusky figures moving near some bushes, and beyond them others apparently moving away from the square. The fire slackened, and it became certain that the Zulu attack had failed: single figures were stealing away in the drifting smoke near the square, and in great numbers the retiring enemy were swarming over the rolling plain towards the hills—a sight which was greeted by an outburst of cheering taken up all round the square, some men enthusiastically throwing their helmets in the air.

For a moment the retreating enemy paused and looked back towards the square, as if in hopes of seeing that formation broken to pursue them, and of finding an opportunity to close hand to hand; but, needless to say, they were destined to disappointment, and the momentary halt was greeted by a short burst of fire. Following the 17th Lancers as they issued forth, I looked back, and remember well the bristling aspect of the red square fringed with rifles and bayonets solidly crowning the rise, and the huge cloud of smoke hanging sombre overhead and rolling slowly to leeward, obstructing the light of the sun, to cast a gigantic shadow over the battlefield, strewn with the weapons of the poor patriots, whose black bodies lay scattered about the trampled grass in every conceivable or inconceivable attitude.

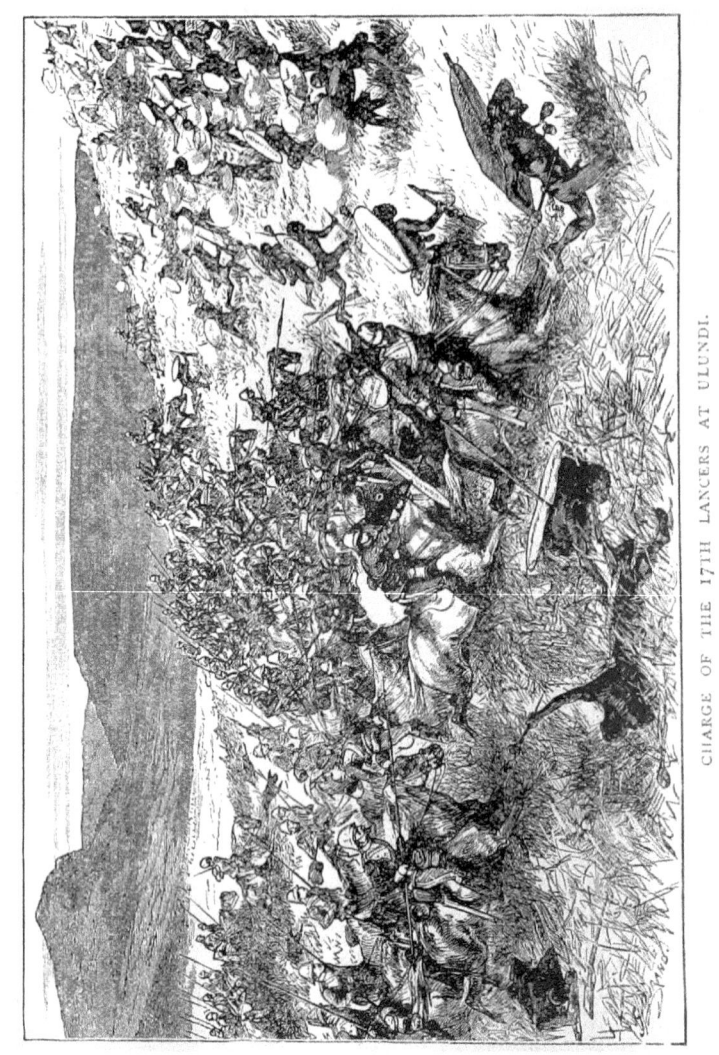

CHARGE OF THE 17TH LANCERS AT ULUNDI.

THE PURSUED TURNED DESPERATELY

Passing in the wake of the lancers, I saw them charge the rearmost Zulus on the nearest hills to the left. The pursued turned desperately and tried to dodge among the horses, sometimes firing amongst them; but the long lances were irresistible, and only the most agile escaped. Then the pursuit slackened, as the overworked horses became blown; but there were others at hand to complete the rout—mounted volunteers whose use of the rifle was more deadly than cold steel, and native auxiliaries whose keen eyes detected fugitives crouching in the grass, and, feeling elated by their ascendency, dashed furiously upon the dreaded Zulu, who not infrequently turned upon his black pursuers.

The repulse was decisive at all points in about three-quarters of an hour from the first infantry fire; and though the general advance was in splendid order, and the crowning attack made with grand courage, yet the Zulus were not anything like so persistent as at the Battle of Ginginhlovu, and I believe that the defeats of Ginginhlovu and Kambula had more than counterbalanced the victories at Isandhlwana and Hlobane, and that they were shaken in the sense of invincibility with which their early successes had inspired them.

That night every man in camp lay down to sleep with a sense of security which had been absent since the crossing of the Blood River, and that same night it might be said that the Zulu War was over, and that Cetywayo's power was a thing of the past already. The smoke of his burning *kraal* hung like a pall over the plain to conceal hundreds of his dead warriors from the great moon which stood calmly and gloriously in the eternal heaven above. Whatever the rights or wrongs which brought on the war, these same brave Zulus died resisting an invasion of their country and homes. Naked savages as they were, let us honour them.

The burning of Ulundi

Isandlwana and Rorke's Drift

By Charles L. Norris-Newman

Dawn broke next day, Wednesday, January the 22nd, with heavy mists on the tops of the Indhlazakazi, Upindo, and Isilulwane Hills. Before daylight our party fell in and stood to their arms, awaiting the promised arrival of the general and reinforcements, who came up shortly afterwards. This force had left the camp at Isandwhlana at 3 a.m. and consisted of a squadron of Mounted Infantry, seven companies of the 2-24th Regiment, and four guns under Colonel Harness, R.A. Lord Chelmsford accompanied the relieving force in person, and was attended by his usual staff and several other officers not specially on duty in camp that day, who had just come out for a ride.

In the meantime, orders had been sent back to Rorke's Drift, to Colonel Durnford, R.E., to bring up his 300 mounted men at once, as also his rocket battery. Having been unable to cross at the Middle Drift, his column was divided and coming slowly up to unite with ours. As daylight progressed, we could see that the main body of the enemy had left the hills in front of us, but their scouts were visible here and there; so, the following preparations were made for surrounding the position.

The Natal Carbineers and Mounted Police under Major Dartnell were started off to get round on the right flank between the position of the enemy and Matyana's stronghold; while the two battalions of the 3rd Regiment N.N.C. were ordered to advance across the valley and sweep right over the hill in front (Isilulwane), which was evidently the key of the position.

In going up, we could notice that the Mounted Infantry

under Colonel Russell, four guns under Colonel Harness, and seven companies of the 2-24th under Colonel Degacher, C.B., were steadily proceeding up the valley on our left along the road which led from our camp farther into the country, with the intention of taming the enemy's right. An ambulance and one other loaded waggon accompanied this force. When the two battalions of the Native Contingent reached the top of the hill after a hard pull up, and no success in "finding ebony," a halt was called. and then within a very few minutes sharp firing was heard, away on the Upindo hill to our right; and upon turning that way, we saw—not two miles off—a lot of our mounted men chasing some Zulus over the hill in a direct line for us.

So, the double was sounded, and away we went to help cut them off. Seeing this, those of the enemy who were not shot left the top of the hill, ran down the sides and took refuge in the caves and rocks abounding. We soon arrived at the spot, and after three hours' work routed all the rest out of their hiding places, shooting many and *assegaing* others. Lieutenant Harford, 99th Regiment, staff officer to Commandant Lonsdale, again distinguished himself by going in alone under a nasty crevice in some stones, shooting two men and capturing another. This officer did the same thing at the attack on Sirayo's strongholds, and would seem to have a charmed life. "May he long keep it!"—was our wish at the time.

The two battalions were then got together, and prepared to march back to the camp, having killed about eighty men. At this point I left them, and galloped across to where the cavalry had re-united, and there heard the history of the whole of their morning's work. It appears that after leaving us that morning they saw a body of the enemy away still farther on the right, among whom were some mounted men, and Major Dartnell gave orders for the *carbineers* and Mounted Police to ride after them.

This they did, and began to open fire (greatly to the astonishment of the Zulus, who stood jeering at them) at eight hundred yards—and even at that distance succeeded in killing one or two.

Seeing this, the enemy fled up the hill as hard as they could; but, as it turned out, not fast enough to escape the men of the *Carbineers*, who, putting their horses to full speed, gained upon them and shot many running. Indeed, I was told by an eye-witness that dead shots were made in this manner at over six hundred yards. Three horses were captured, and the stern chase continued until they met the men of the Native Contingent, when they returned, leaving it to their sable allies to finish up the business.

Over sixty were then killed, and we only know of one man who escaped. Matyana himself was nearly caught by Captain Shepstone, N.C., who chased him for miles on horseback, and was close to him, when he jumped off his horse and dropped over a steep *krantz*. The horse was brought into camp. The mounted men under Major Dartnell then had tea and biscuits, and awaited the coming up of the general and staff for farther orders.

As scattered bodies of the enemy, apparently falling back on their main supports, had been seen by the other attacking parties, a general advance was ordered by Lord Chelmsford, who remained with the infantry and guns, which continued advancing up the valley to the left of the Isilulwane hill; while Colonel Russell with the Mounted Infantry went on still farther to turn the right of the Isipezi hill, and then to act as circumstances might require.

The idea did not seem to have occurred to any one that the enemy were carrying out a preconcerted plan. At ten o'clock the general and his staff made a halt at the top of the valley for breakfast; and shortly afterwards Captain Buller, Rifle Brigade, A.D.C., rode up with the information that the mounted men were engaged on the extreme right; at the same time the news first arrived that large bodies of the enemy were seen on the left of our camp. The general then ordered the l-3rd N.N.C., under Commandant Browne, to retire on the camp, and scatter any small bodies of the enemy that might be found hovering about between us and the camp.

At 11 a.m., Lord Chelmsford then rode away towards the

LORD CHELMSFORD

right, sending two companies of the 2-24th over the hill; and the rest went back by the road they had come, until they arrived at the place where it branched off to the site of our proposed new camping ground, to which they at once proceeded, as escort to the guns. Those officers who had accompanied the general for a ride only here left him, and unfortunately for themselves returned to camp.

An escort of ten mounted infantry went with these officers, among whom were Captain Allan Gardner, 14th Hussars, Lieutenant McDougall, R.E., and Lieutenants Dyer, 1-24th, and Griffiths, 2-24th. After passing over the Isilulwane hill, the General proceeded along the Upindo until he came up with the Mounted Police, Natal Carbineers and Native Battalion, who had been engaged with Matyana and his followers.

The general only remained for a short time, to receive from Major Dartnell his report on the morning's work, and then left us, with instructions to return two miles farther back, to the head of the Amange gorge, and there remain; his intention being that the camp at Isandwhlana should be struck that afternoon (Wednesday), and the entire force moved forward to the spot selected as our halting-ground. This intention, it is almost needless to add, was unhappily never carried into effect. But our orders were at once acted upon, and on our arrival, we found the staff already there, looking through their field-glasses at some large bodies of Zulus, who were about ten miles away, massed in proximity to the camp.

This was at about half an hour past noon; and it was then that the first uneasy suspicion was aroused in our minds, that some important, possibly sinister, events were perhaps in progress at the camp. Mr. Longcast, the general's interpreter, learned from one of the prisoners that an immense army had been expected to arrive that very day from Ulundi; and from the enumeration of the different regiments composing it, the numbers of that force were variously estimated, by those familiar with them, at from 20,000 to 25,000. Suddenly, during his cross-examination of other prisoners, the sound of artillery-fire was distinctly heard in the direction of the camp; and the Zulus immediately said, "Do you hear that? There is fighting going on at the camp."

This was at once reported to the general, who was by this time some way down the hill, towards the spot, near the Amange stream, where the Mounted Police and *Carbineers* were already off-saddled. Remaining there only for a very few moments, he passed on to the lower part of the Amange, where the road crosses, to select a site for the new camp. At this juncture one of our mounted natives came galloping down from the opposite ridge, whence the camp could be seen, and reported to a staff-officer that an attack was being made on the camp, as he had seen heavy firing and heard the big guns.

On this being reported to Lord Chelmsford he at once galloped up to the crest of the hill, accompanied by his staff, and on arrival every field-glass was levelled at the camp. The sun was shining brightly on the white tents, which were plainly visible, but all seemed quiet. No signs of firing, or of an engagement could be seen, and although bodies of men moving about could be distinguished, yet they were not unnaturally supposed to be our own troops. The time was now 1.45 p.m. and not the faintest idea of disaster occurred to us. It was believed that an attack on the camp had been made and repulsed, as those who knew the arrangements previously made for its defence had every right and reason to assume.

Some time was passed on the ridge, and it was not until a quarter to three that the general turned his horse's head downwards to the Amange stream. After some time had been passed on the site marked out for the new camping ground orders were given for Captain Shepstone and his volunteers to return to the camp and ascertain the position of affairs there, and what had occurred.

I joined them, and we had not proceeded very far on the road when we met a mounted messenger, who had been sent off by Colonel Pulleine with a note to Lord Chelmsford, to inform him that the camp was attacked by large numbers of Zulus, and requesting him to return at once with all the forces at his command. Upon this we halted to await the arrival of the general, who quickly came up with us, accompanied by the Mounted Infantry, and proceeded up the valley with us to reconnoitre. At this time, we had travelled about three miles on our return, and had passed Colonel Harness with his four guns, accompanied by a detachment of the 2-24th, the ambulance and a waggon, and the main body of the Mounted Infantry, all on their way to the new encampment.

At this moment a mounted man was seen approaching, and speedily recognised as Commandant Lonsdale, who proved to be the bearer of the most dreadful news. Those who were present when he told his terrible tidings to Lord Chelmsford will never forget the scene, nor their feelings at the time, as they exchanged looks of amazement, grief, and horror.

It appeared that in pursuing a mounted Zulu he had become separated from his corps, and had therefore ridden quietly back to the camp at Isandwhlana. On arriving within 300 yards of it, at about 2 p.m., he found large masses of the enemy surrounding it, and in conflict with our troops. He had but just time, on discovering the state of matters, to turn and fly for his life: several shots were fired after him, and he was chased by many Zulus.

But owing, fortunately, to the stoutness and pluck of his well-known little pony, "Dot," he succeeded in escaping the pursuit, and rejoined his regiment, also marching back in false security, and utter ignorance, like all the rest of us, of the frightful catastrophe which had occurred not five miles away. For although, as stated, the sound of artillery-fire, and even the rattle of musketry, had been heard during the morning, yet they were attributed to some skirmishing only, and no one even had a thought of the fatal truth.

So soon as Commandant Lonsdale's tale was told, orders were sent back, by Major Gossett, *A.D.C.*, for the rest of the column to return at once; and meanwhile we halted, awaiting their arrival with unspeakable impatience and anxiety. In order, if possible, to gain farther information, mounted patrols were detached, in skirmishing order, to the crests of the adjoining ridges, to watch the progress of events. As they came in, we could only learn that the enemy were rapidly increasing in numbers, and seemed to have beaten our troops, and to be burning the tents and taking away large quantities of stores, waggons, oxen and horses.

This news served to increase our maddening impatience, and the miserable anxiety with which we awaited the oncoming of our supports. This was further enhanced by the report of a small scouting party of mounted men, who were sent forward with orders to approach as near as possible to the camp. On their return, they brought the intelligence that nearly all firing had ceased, and everything was in possession of the enemy, who held in great force what was almost our only road back to Natal.

It was universally felt that to attempt an advance with only two battalions of the Native Contingent and a few jaded cavalry would be rash and foolhardy in the extreme. At the same time the news was scarcely accepted as true; or at least we hoped it might prove to be only partially so; and that our troops had simply been driven to fall back on Rorke's Drift, by the superior numbers of the enemy.

It was quite four o'clock when the rest of our reconnoitring column rejoined us, and the order of march for our whole force was established as follows:—The four guns were placed in the centre, with a half battalion of the 2-24th extended in line on each flank, that on the right being commanded by Colonel Degacher, that on the left by Major Black; on either side of them were eight companies of the 3rd N.N.C.; and the cavalry outside of all, on the flanks; Major Dartnell, in command of the Mounted Police and Volunteers, on the left; and Colonel Russell, with his Mounted Infantry, on the right. The ambulance and waggons followed the guns, with a small guard closing np the rear.

Before the march was commenced the general briefly addressed the men, saying that the camp had fallen into the hands of the enemy, who had captured it in overwhelming force during our absence; but that he relied upon them to retake it, and so reopen our communications with Natal. Then the advance was made in the above order—with fear in our hearts as to the events that might have taken place, but nevertheless with a stern determination to recapture the position, even in the increasing darkness, and whatever might be the cost.

When we arrived within two miles of the camp, advanced guards were sent forward, but nothing was seen of the enemy. Our route was continued in the same order and with all precautions; the daylight dying away more and more, until, when the water-wash to the south of the camp was crossed, it was as dark as it ever became throughout that memorable night. At a distance of within a mile, where the ground rose to the site of the camp, we could see, by the shadows against the horizon, on the top of the neck of land, where our road ran back to the Bashee Valley, and so on to Rorke's Drift, that the enemy had dragged numerous waggons, so as to place a sort of barrier across our only road back.

And from behind this we thought we could hear the hoarse cries of the enemy, and the rattle of their *knobkerries* and *assegais* against their shields. A halt was therefore made to allow the guns to pour four rounds of shrapnel into the barricade, when the advance was resumed. Meanwhile Major Black received orders to gain possession, at all risks, of the *kopje* on the left of the ridge; as those holding it would then be enabled to protect our flank effectually, and to command the ridge itself with a destructive fire. As the gallant major moved off in the dark on this hazardous errand, apparently one of almost certain death, I heard him call out to his men, "No firing, but only one volley, boys, and then give them the cold steel."

After a short advance by the main body a second halt took place, and the shrapnel-fire was repeated. Afterwards all was silence, and we resumed our onward march. The 2-24th on the right were ordered to fire a few rounds, with the object of drawing the fire of the enemy, if any, but fruitlessly; and then, in silence and darkness, we moved on once more.

A little farther on, and we began to stumble over dead bodies in every direction, and in some places, especially where from the formation of the ground there was a ditch or anything like shelter, the men were found lying thick and close, as though they had fought there till their ammunition was exhausted, and then been surrounded and slaughtered. When within a few hundred yards of the top of the ridge, with the large and grotesque form of the Isandwhlana Mountain looming up in front of us, and showing clearly against the sky in the dusk of evening, we heard a ringing British cheer from hundreds of throats.

We thus learnt that Major Black and his men of the 2-24th had gained the *kopje* without any resistance, and therefore that the enemy had retired still farther, though between us and Rorke's Drift. It was 8 or 9 p.m. by the time our little force had ascended the ridge: we received orders to bivouac where and as we were, on the field of slaughter, and only to move forward by daylight in the morning. Such precautions as were possible were taken to guard against a surprise; for it was known that a large force was following in the rear; and the victorious enemy were believed to be in close proximity to our front and flanks.

But oh! how dreadful were those weary hours that followed! while all had to watch and wait, through the darkness, with what patience we could muster, for the dawn of day; with the knowledge that we were standing and lying amid and surrounded by the corpses of our late comrades—though in what fearful numbers we then but little knew. Many a vow of vengeance was breathed in the stillness of the night; and many and deep were the sobs that came from the breasts of men who, perhaps, had never sobbed before, at discovering, even by that dim light, the bodies of dear friends, brutally massacred, stripped of all clothing, disembowelled, mutilated, and in some cases decapitated.

How that terrible night passed with us I fancy few would care to tell, even if they could recall it. For my own part, I felt both reckless and despairing—reckless at the almost certain prospect of an overwhelming attack by the enemy, flushed with victory—despairing, because of the melancholy scene of horror which I felt awaited us at daybreak. During the night we noticed fires constantly burning in all the surrounding hills; and in particular one bright blaze riveted our attention throughout, as it seemed to be near Rorke's Drift, and we feared for the safety of those left in that small place, knowing how utterly powerless we were to aid them in any way before morning. Happily, in this instance, our fears were vain.

After lying down for a while close to the general and his staff, I arose at about an hour before daylight, for the purpose of taking a quiet look around, to see the state of matters for myself, and recognise what bodies I could. Nothing but a sense of duty could have induced me to undertake the task, or sustained me in its execution so as to go through with it. Not even on the recent battlefields of Europe, though hundreds were lying where now I saw only tens, was there over a more sickening or heart-rending sight!

The corpses of our poor soldiers, whites and natives, lay thick upon the ground in dusters, together with dead and mutilated horses, oxen and mules, shot and stabbed in every position and manner; and the whole intermingled with the fragments of our commissariat waggons, broken and wrecked, and rifled of their contents, such as flour, sugar, tea, biscuits, mealies, oats, &c., &c., the debris being all scattered about, and wasted as in pure wantonness on the ground. The dead bodies of the men lay as they had fallen, but mostly with only their boots and shirts on, or perhaps a pair of trousers or a remnant of a coat, with just sufficient means of recognition to determine to which branch of the Service they had belonged.

In many instances they lay with sixty or seventy empty cartridge cases surrounding them, thus showing that they had fought to the very last, and only succumbed and fallen, after doing their duty without flinching, and when all means of resistance were exhausted. It seemed to me, at the time, that it was really wonderful that so small a force had been able to maintain such a desperate resistance for so long. There were, indeed, only about 900 men in camp, exclusive of our natives, who ran away, and of Colonel Durnford's mounted men, under Captain Barton; and

AFTER ISANDLWANA–

yet, fighting in the open, without defensive works, protection or cover, they kept at bay for hours the almost overwhelming army of Zulus, by whom they were attacked and surrounded.

Captain Barton subsequently told me that his mounted men really fought well at their first charge, and until all their ammunition was exhausted; they were then compelled to fall back on the camp, where they sought for a fresh supply of ammunition. Unfortunately, this was refused them by the officer in charge, who said it would all be required by the infantry themselves. This was assuredly a fatal error of judgment, inasmuch as a large quantity of ammunition unused fell into the hands of the enemy, together with more than 1,000 Martini-Henry rifles and carbines.

Perhaps, however, though the defence might have been prolonged, the disastrous issue could not have been averted, considering the strength of the enemy. So far as I could judge, from what I saw through my field-glass, combined with all the reliable information which could possibly be obtained at the time, and careful computation, the line of Zulu warriors, which came down from the hills on the left, must have extended over a length of nearly three miles, and consisted of more than 15,000 men.

And another large body, of at least 5,000, was held in reserve, remaining on the crest of the slope and taking no part in the first onslaught. They took part in the work of spoil and plunder at the camp, and aided in driving off the captured cattle and such waggons as had not been wrecked. Most of the bodies of their dead were also removed by them in the waggons, so that not many were found by us on the field; this makes it difficult to form any accurate estimate of the total loss on their side, which must have been considerable.

Assuming that our troops had seventy rounds each, and allowing for the effective execution of many rounds of shrapnel and case from the two guns, as well as the rockets, discharged into the dense masses at close quarters, I think the Zulu loss may fairly be set down at not far short of 2,000, an estimate which has been considered low by military men well qualified to judge.

I had scarcely returned from my melancholy round, when, just as daylight began to appear, preparations for the advance were completed, and the word was given to march. Formed in fours, not in line this time, we proceeded rapidly on our return route, with strong advanced and rear guards, and feeling well on our flanks. On nearing the farther side of the plain, where the neck of land gives access to the Bashee valley, we saw in the distance on our left a returning Zulu *impi*, numbering many thousands. Judging from the numerous evidences of burning *kraals* bordering the Buffalo River itself, we concluded that this was a part of the victorious army which had set out from Isandwhlana, attacked the post at Rorke's Drift, and were now on their way back to Ulundi, after raiding the Border.

This sight served to intensify our anxiety, and caused us to hurry onwards. We quickly reached the brow of the hill overlooking the Buffalo River and Rorke's Drift, with our previous camping ground on the opposite bank; but the sight of buildings in flames at the station by no means allayed our fears. Before we quite reached the river, I carefully examined the house at Rorke's Drift through my field-glass, and thought I could distinguish the figures of men on parts of the wall and roof of the large building, and one of them seemed to be waving a flag. The attention of the general having been called to this, Colonel Russell, with some of his mounted infantry and myself, at once crossed the river and galloped up to the station at full speed.

Much to our delight and relief, we were greeted with a hearty English cheer, showing that here at least no irreparable disaster had befallen. We quickly dismounted, and found the place had been temporarily defended by a barricade of empty biscuit-boxes and mealies in sacks, while outside numerous bodies of dead Zulus were lying all around. The little garrison, it appeared, had received timely warning from the fugitives escaped from the camp at Isandwhlana, and they were thus enabled to make some slight preparations for the anticipated assault, so that they successfully withstood, and repulsed with severe loss to the enemy, a body of over 4,000 Zulus, that had commenced the attack on

RELIEF OF RORKE'S DRIFT

them at five on the previous (Wednesday) evening, and continued almost unintermittingly till daybreak, only retiring upon the approach of our little column.

The small garrison consisted of only about 130 men, under Lieutenant Chard, R.E., and Lieutenant Bromhead, 2-24th. Major Spalding, D.A.Q.M.G., had been left in command of the post, but had gone away to Helpmakaar late on the Tuesday afternoon preceding. The following officers were also present at the post and rendered material aid in the defence: Dr. Reynolds, l-24th, Lieutenant Agender, l-3rd N.N.C., Messrs. Dunne, Dalton, and Byrne, of the Commissariat Department, as also the Rev. Mr. Smith, Protestant Chaplain to No. 3 Column.

It seems that several parties of men, escaping from the scene of the massacre at Isandwhlana, some of them strong in numbers, passed by Rorke's Drift; but it must be said, much to their discredit, they would not remain to aid the little garrison, but continued their flight to Helpmakaar. The conflagration which we had seen was in a detached building, used as a hospital, at some little distance away from the house; this, though at first defended, could not be held, and had therefore been evacuated.

The rest of the Mounted Infantry, and the general with his staff, speedily also arrived at the station; and the gallant defenders, on relating the particulars of their heroic resistance, were warmly commended and deservedly congratulated. The remainder of the column in the meantime crossed the river and encamped temporarily close by. Shortly afterwards, by the general's orders, the entire force was set to work to clear the ground around the station of all cover for an enemy's attack, to reconstruct and strengthen the barricade, and to mount the four guns, one at each corner. The roof of the house, being of thatch, was also stripped from it, to prevent farther peril of fire.

The two battalions of the N.N.C. were posted on the large hill at the back, to prevent any enemy occupying it to fire down on the station, and also to keep guard on the river. These preparations were necessary, as precautions against any possible attack, as the general had decided to remain for the time at Rorke's

Drift; and they occupied the whole morning. Not till they were completed were the rations served out. It will readily be conceived what a boon this was at last, to men who had been out for two days and nights, who had had during that time absolutely nothing to eat but a little biscuit and tinned meat, and nothing to drink except bad water, while undergoing the fatigues of marching and skirmishing, and the wretched anxiety of such a miserable bivouac as our last.

Colonel Russell was then sent on, with a mounted escort, in order to see if the road was open up to Helpmakaar, and to learn what had been and was being done there. During his absence, however, three officers arrived, belonging to the 1st N.N.G. under Major Bengough (part of what had been Colonel Durnford's force). They had ridden down from Helpmakaar, and found the roads open and clear of the enemy. No attack had, up to that time, been made upon that station, which was well guarded, a *laager* having been formed. Small parties and scouts of the enemy had been seen in the valleys below and on the surrounding hills.

We also learnt, half-an-hour later, that the country to the north was free of the Zulus, a party of the Buffalo Border Guard having ridden over from Fort Pine. Trivial as these items of intelligence may now appear, they were at the time significant and useful to us, by restoring hope to our hearts, as indicating that no attack by any overwhelming force of the enemy was to be apprehended, and that there would be time to reorganise the column and repair our loss of men and means.

For my part, on considering the serious nature of the reverse which our troops had suffered, and the great importance of transmitting full and correct particulars, I at once resolved to start that same evening, and ride straight back to Pieter Maritzburg, so as to be in time to telegraph the news to Cape Town, for despatch by the mail-steamer for England of the following Monday.

This I was happily enabled to effect, and so give the colonial people the earliest trustworthy intelligence as to the list of killed and missing from the Headquarters Column. Having made my determination known, undertook to be the bearer of any despatches, messages, or telegrams, and received a great many from all ranks, from His Excellency downwards. I made all my preparations as rapidly possible, as reports had come in from some of Commandant Lonsdale's native scouts to the effect that Zulus were crossing the river at a point lower down, and it was considered possible at the station at Rorke's Drift might again be attacked in force that night.

I therefore took my leave of Lord Chelmsford—who, in spite of his grief at the recent disaster, was still thoughtful enough to devote a few friendly words to me—and saying goodbye to all those who had happily come out of that "Valley of Death" with me, I galloped off. Though sore at heart at parting from those with whom I had gone through so much, I was not sorry to find myself on the road to Pieter Maritzburg, with news of importance to all interested in the officers and men of our column.

I may appropriately close this narrative of our mischance by a quotation from the letter of a staff-officer, written on these events:—

> There was reason to believe that the Zulu Army consisted of the Undi corps, including the Tulwana, Nkonkone, Ndhlonhlo, and Ndhluyengwe regiments, about 4,000 strong; the Umcityu, including the Unqakamatye and Umtulisazwe regiments, about 6,000 strong; the Nkobamakosi regiment, about 4,000 strong; the Inkulutyane, including the Umsikaba and Unddududu regiments, 2,500 strong; and the Nokenke, 2,000 strong; or an aggregate of about 18,500 men in regiments. Besides this there were at least another 5,000 men belonging to various tribes and head men, making the whole force employed against No. 3 Column on the 22nd inst. about 23,000 to 24,000 men. Of this number the last named were ordered to show themselves as much as possible, and induce as many of our troops to go in pursuit of them as they could, avoiding at the same time actual fighting—this they did to perfec-

tion. A force of some 15,000 men was moved up from the Ibabinango mountain during the night of the 21st inst., a distance of about 25 miles, not *en masse,* but in small parties. On arriving to the left of our position they lay down as they were, fires and speaking being strictly prohibited. Another body, about 3,000 or 4,000 strong, was ordered to watch the road to Rorke's Drift, and follow up all those who might escape that way, and I believe that had our men followed the waggon road instead of going straight across country, hardly one would have come out alive.

We know how well carried out, tactically speaking, were the Zulu generals' strategic arrangements. In the attack on the camp there was no hurry or excitement on their part. They first outflanked and surrounded it, and then, and not till then, did they give way to their natural impetuosity and charge with the *assegai.* No soldier can, I think, fail to admire and respect the soldier-like qualities thus displayed by the enemy, much as his hatred and contempt may be excited by the brutal and savage characteristics they otherwise exhibited, and in the future the Zulu Army will command that amount of precaution and respect which is necessary before it can be conquered.

ALSO FROM LEONAUR
AVAILABLE IN SOFTCOVER OR HARDCOVER WITH DUST JACKET

THE FALL OF THE MOGHUL EMPIRE OF HINDUSTAN *by H. G. Keene*—By the beginning of the nineteenth century, as British and Indian armies under Lake and Wellesley dominated the scene, a little over half a century of conflict brought the Moghul Empire to its knees.

LADY SALE'S AFGHANISTAN *by Florentia Sale*—An Indomitable Victorian Lady's Account of the Retreat from Kabul During the First Afghan War.

THE CAMPAIGN OF MAGENTA AND SOLFERINO 1859 *by Harold Carmichael Wylly*—The Decisive Conflict for the Unification of Italy.

FRENCH'S CAVALRY CAMPAIGN *by J. G. Maydon*—A Special Correspondent's View of British Army Mounted Troops During the Boer War.

CAVALRY AT WATERLOO *by Sir Evelyn Wood*—British Mounted Troops During the Campaign of 1815.

THE SUBALTERN *by George Robert Gleig*—The Experiences of an Officer of the 85th Light Infantry During the Peninsular War.

NAPOLEON AT BAY, 1814 *by F. Loraine Petre*—The Campaigns to the Fall of the First Empire.

NAPOLEON AND THE CAMPAIGN OF 1806 *by Colonel Vachée*—The Napoleonic Method of Organisation and Command to the Battles of Jena & Auerstädt.

THE COMPLETE ADVENTURES IN THE CONNAUGHT RANGERS *by William Grattan*—The 88th Regiment during the Napoleonic Wars by a Serving Officer.

BUGLER AND OFFICER OF THE RIFLES *by William Green & Harry Smith*—With the 95th (Rifles) during the Peninsular & Waterloo Campaigns of the Napoleonic Wars.

NAPOLEONIC WAR STORIES *by Sir Arthur Quiller-Couch*—Tales of soldiers, spies, battles & sieges from the Peninsular & Waterloo campaigns.

CAPTAIN OF THE 95TH (RIFLES) *by Jonathan Leach*—An officer of Wellington's sharpshooters during the Peninsular, South of France and Waterloo campaigns of the Napoleonic wars.

RIFLEMAN COSTELLO *by Edward Costello*—The adventures of a soldier of the 95th (Rifles) in the Peninsular & Waterloo Campaigns of the Napoleonic wars.

AVAILABLE ONLINE AT **www.leonaur.com**
AND FROM ALL GOOD BOOK STORES

ALSO FROM LEONAUR

AVAILABLE IN SOFTCOVER OR HARDCOVER WITH DUST JACKET

THE 9TH—THE KING'S (LIVERPOOL REGIMENT) IN THE GREAT WAR 1914 - 1918 by Enos H. G. Roberts—Mersey to mud—war and Liverpool men.

THE GAMBARDIER by Mark Severn—The experiences of a battery of Heavy artillery on the Western Front during the First World War.

FROM MESSINES TO THIRD YPRES by Thomas Floyd—A personal account of the First World War on the Western front by a 2/5th Lancashire Fusilier.

THE IRISH GUARDS IN THE GREAT WAR - VOLUME 1 by Rudyard Kipling—Edited and Compiled from Their Diaries and Papers—The First Battalion.

THE IRISH GUARDS IN THE GREAT WAR - VOLUME 1 by Rudyard Kipling—Edited and Compiled from Their Diaries and Papers—The Second Battalion.

ARMOURED CARS IN EDEN by K. Roosevelt—An American President's son serving in Rolls Royce armoured cars with the British in Mesopatamia & with the American Artillery in France during the First World War.

CHASSEUR OF 1914 by Marcel Dupont—Experiences of the twilight of the French Light Cavalry by a young officer during the early battles of the great war in Europe.

TROOP HORSE & TRENCH by R.A. Lloyd—The experiences of a British Lifeguardsman of the household cavalry fighting on the western front during the First World War 1914-18.

THE EAST AFRICAN MOUNTED RIFLES by C.J. Wilson—Experiences of the campaign in the East African bush during the First World War.

THE LONG PATROL by George Berrie—A Novel of Light Horsemen from Gallipoli to the Palestine campaign of the First World War.

THE FIGHTING CAMELIERS by Frank Reid—The exploits of the Imperial Camel Corps in the desert and Palestine campaigns of the First World War.

STEEL CHARIOTS IN THE DESERT by S. C. Rolls—The first world war experiences of a Rolls Royce armoured car driver with the Duke of Westminster in Libya and in Arabia with T.E. Lawrence.

WITH THE IMPERIAL CAMEL CORPS IN THE GREAT WAR by Geoffrey Inchbald—The story of a serving officer with the British 2nd battalion against the Senussi and during the Palestine campaign.

AVAILABLE ONLINE AT **www.leonaur.com**
AND FROM ALL GOOD BOOK STORES

ALSO FROM LEONAUR
AVAILABLE IN SOFTCOVER OR HARDCOVER WITH DUST JACKET

ESCAPE FROM THE FRENCH by Edward Boys—A Young Royal Navy Midshipman's Adventures During the Napoleonic War.

THE VOYAGE OF H.M.S. PANDORA by Edward Edwards R. N. & George Hamilton, edited by Basil Thomson—In Pursuit of the Mutineers of the Bounty in the South Seas—1790-1791.

MEDUSA by J. B. Henry Savigny and Alexander Correard and Charlotte-Adélaïde Dard —Narrative of a Voyage to Senegal in 1816 & The Sufferings of the Picard Family After the Shipwreck of the Medusa.

THE SEA WAR OF 1812 VOLUME 1 by A. T. Mahan—A History of the Maritime Conflict.

THE SEA WAR OF 1812 VOLUME 2 by A. T. Mahan—A History of the Maritime Conflict.

WETHERELL OF H. M. S. HUSSAR by John Wetherell—The Recollections of an Ordinary Seaman of the Royal Navy During the Napoleonic Wars.

THE NAVAL BRIGADE IN NATAL by C. R. N. Burne—With the Guns of H. M. S. Terrible & H. M. S. Tartar during the Boer War 1899-1900.

THE VOYAGE OF H. M. S. BOUNTY by William Bligh—The True Story of an 18th Century Voyage of Exploration and Mutiny.

SHIPWRECK! by William Gilly—The Royal Navy's Disasters at Sea 1793-1849.

KING'S CUTTERS AND SMUGGLERS: 1700-1855 by E. Keble Chatterton—A unique period of maritime history-from the beginning of the eighteenth to the middle of the nineteenth century when British seamen risked all to smuggle valuable goods from wool to tea and spirits from and to the Continent.

CONFEDERATE BLOCKADE RUNNER by John Wilkinson—The Personal Recollections of an Officer of the Confederate Navy.

NAVAL BATTLES OF THE NAPOLEONIC WARS by W. H. Fitchett—Cape St. Vincent, the Nile, Cadiz, Copenhagen, Trafalgar & Others.

PRISONERS OF THE RED DESERT by R. S. Gwatkin-Williams—The Adventures of the Crew of the Tara During the First World War.

U-BOAT WAR 1914-1918 by James B. Connolly/Karl von Schenk—Two Contrasting Accounts from Both Sides of the Conflict at Sea D uring the Great War.

AVAILABLE ONLINE AT **www.leonaur.com**
AND FROM ALL GOOD BOOK STORES